Quick Colourful Quilts
for Babies and Toddlers

Quick Colourful Quilts

for

Babies

and

Toddlers

Edited by Rosemary Wilkinson

First published in 2006 by
New Holland Publishers (UK) Ltd
London I Cape Town I Sydney I Auckland
www.newhollandpublishers.com

Garfield House, 86-88 Edgware Road, London W2 2EA

80 McKenzie Street, Cape Town 8001, South Africa

Unit 4, 14 Aquatic Drive, Frenchs Forest, NSW 2086, Australia

218 Lake Road, Northcote, Auckland, New Zealand

2 4 6 8 10 9 7 5 3 1

ISBN 1 184537 077 5

Editor: Rosemary Wilkinson
Design: Frances de Rees
Photographs: Shona Wood
Illustrations: Carrie Hill
Template diagrams: Stephen Dew
Production: Hazel Kirkman

Reproduction by Pica Digital PTE Ltd, Singapore
Printed and bound in Malaysia by
Times Offset (M) Sdn Bhd

Contents

MATERIALS

PATCHWORK FABRICS

The easiest fabrics to work with for patchwork are closely woven, 100% cotton. They "cling" together making a stable unit for cutting and stitching, they don't fray too readily and they press well. Quilting shops and suppliers stock a fantastic range in both solid colours and prints, usually in 45 in/115 cm widths, and most of the quilts in this book are based on these cottons.

BACKING AND BINDING FABRICS

The backing and binding fabrics should be the same type and weight as the fabrics used in the patchwork top. They can be a coordinating colour or a strong contrast. You could also be adven-

Waddings left to right: silk, cotton, 2 oz cream polyester, black cotton, 80%/20% cotton/polyester, wool, grey and white polyester

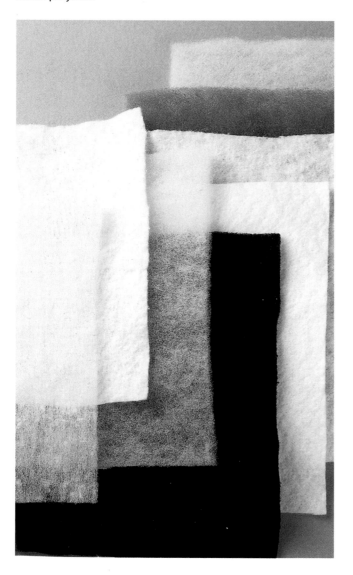

turous and piece the backing, too, to make a reversible quilt. In either case, the colour of the binding needs to work with both the top and the backing fabric designs.

WADDING

Various types of wadding are available in cotton, polyester, wool, silk or mixed fibres. They can be bought in pre-cut sizes suitable for cot quilts and different sizes of bed quilts or in lengths cut from a bolt. They also come in different weights or "lofts" depending on how padded you want the quilt to be. Lightweight polyester wadding is the most commonly used, but some wool or cotton types are more suited to hand quilting. For babies, natural fibres are recommended, but if you're making a playmat or picnic mat which would need constant washing, you would probably choose polyester. Quilts are not recommended at all for babies under six months. Some waddings need to be closely quilted to prevent them from bunching up; others can be quilted up to 8 in/20 cm apart. Follow the manufacturer's instructions if in doubt.

QUANTITIES AND FABRIC PREPARATION

The quantities given at the beginning of each project have been calculated to allow for a bit extra – just in case! A few of the quilts combine cutting down the length of the fabric with cutting across the width. This is to make the most economical use of fabric or to obtain border pieces cut in one piece.

Unless otherwise stated, any 10 in/25 cm requirement is the "long" quarter – the full width of the fabric – and not the "fat" quarter, which is a piece 18 x 22 in/50 x 56 cm.

All fabrics should be washed prior to use in order to wash out any excess dye and to avoid fabrics shrinking at different rates. Before they are completely dry, iron the fabrics and fold them selvage to selvage – as they were originally on the bolt – in preparation for cutting.

TECHNIQUES

ROTARY CUTTING

The basis of rotary cutting is that fabric is cut first in strips – usually across the width of the fabric, then cross-cut into squares or rectangles. Unless otherwise stated, fabric is used folded selvage to selvage, wrong sides together, as it has come off the bolt.

MAKING THE EDGE STRAIGHT

Before any accurate cutting can be done, you must first make sure the cut edge of the fabric is at right angles to the selvages.

1 Place the folded fabric on the cutting mat with the fabric smoothed out, the selvages exactly aligned at the top and the bulk of the fabric on the side that is not your cutting hand. Place the ruler on the fabric next to the cut edge, aligning the horizontal lines on the ruler with the fold and with the selvages.

2 Place your non-cutting hand on the ruler to hold it straight and apply pressure. Keep the hand holding the ruler in line with the cutting hand. Place the cutter on the mat just below the fabric and up against the ruler. Start cutting by running the cutter upwards and right next to the edge of the ruler (pic 1).

pic 1

3 When the cutter becomes level with your extended fingertips, stop cutting but leave the cutter in position and carefully move the hand holding the ruler further along the ruler to keep the applied pressure in the area where the cutting is taking place. Continue cutting and moving the steadying hand as necessary until you have cut completely across the fabric. As soon as the cut is complete, close the safety shield on the cutter. If you run out of cutting mat, you will need to reposition the fabric, but this is not ideal as it can bring the fabric out of alignment.

4 Open out the narrow strip of fabric just cut off. Check to make sure that a "valley" or a "hill" has not appeared at the point of the fold on the edge just cut; it should be perfectly straight. If it is not, the fabric was not folded correctly. Fold the fabric again, making sure that this time the selvages are exactly aligned. Make another cut to straighten the edge and check again.

CUTTING STRIPS

The next stage is to cut strips across the width of the fabric. To do this, change the position of the fabric to the opposite side of the board, then use the measurements on the ruler to cut the strips.

1 Place the fabric on the cutting mat on the side of your cutting hand. Place the ruler on the mat so that it overlaps the fabric.

Align the cut edge of the fabric with the vertical line on the ruler that corresponds to the measurement that you wish to cut. The horizontal lines on the ruler should be aligned with the folded edge and the selvage of the fabric.

2 As before, place one hand on the ruler to apply pressure while cutting the fabric with the other hand (pic 2).

pic 2

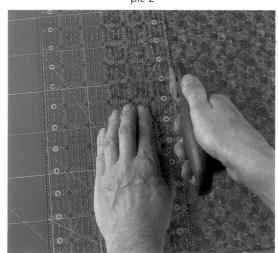

CROSS-CUTTING

The strips can now be cut into smaller units, described as cross-cutting, and these units are sometimes sub-cut into triangles.

Squares

1 Place the strip just cut on the cutting mat with the longest edge horizontal to you and most of the fabric on the side of the non-cutting hand. Cut off the selvages in the same way in which you straightened the fabric edge at the start of the process.

2 Now place the strip on the opposite side of the mat and cut across (cross-cut) the strip using the same measurement on the rule as used for cutting the strip; ensure that the horizontal lines of the ruler align with the horizontal edges of the fabric. You have now created two squares of the required measurement (pic 3). Repeat as required.

pic 3

Rectangles

1 First cut a strip to one of the required side measurements for the rectangle. Remove the selvages.
2 Turn the strip to the horizontal position as for the squares.
3 Cross-cut this strip using the other side measurement required for the rectangle. Again, ensure that the horizontal lines of the ruler align with the horizontal cut edges of the strip.

Wide Strips

Placing two rulers side by side can aid the cutting of extra-wide strips. If you don't have two rulers, place the fabric on the cutting mat in the correct position for cutting. Align the cut edge of the fabric with one of the vertical lines running completely across the cutting board, and the folded edge with one of the horizontal lines. If the measurement does not fall on one of the lines on the cutting mat, use the ruler in conjunction with the cutting mat.

Multi-strip Units

This two-stage method of cutting strips, then cross-cutting into squares or rectangles, can also be used to speed up the cutting of multi-strip units to provide strip blocks, such as those used for the Tic-tac-toe quilt on page 26.
1 Cut the required number and size of strips and stitch together as per the instructions for the block/quilt you are making. Press the seams and check that they are smooth on the right side of the strip unit with no pleats or wrinkles.

2 Place the unit right side up in the horizontal position on the cutting mat. Align the horizontal lines on the ruler with the longer cut edges of the strips and with the seam lines just created (pic 4). If, after you have cut a few cross-cuts, the lines on the ruler do not line up with the cut edges as well as the seam lines, re-cut the end to straighten it before cutting any more units.

pic 4

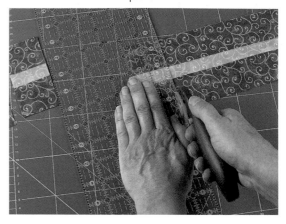

ROTARY CUTTING TRIANGLES

Squares can be divided into either two or four triangles, called half-square or quarter-square triangles. Both sizes of triangle can be quickly cut using the rotary cutter or they can be made even faster by a quick piecing method described on page 88.

Cutting Half-square Triangles

1 Cut the fabric into strips of the correct depth and remove the selvages.
2 Cross-cut the strips into squares of the correct width.
3 Align the 45° angle line on the ruler with the sides of the square and place the edge of the ruler so that it goes diagonally across the square from corner to corner. Cut the square on this diagonal, creating two half-square triangles (pic 5).

pic 5

Cutting Quarter-square Triangles

1 Cut the fabric into strips of the correct depth and remove the selvages.

2 Cross-cut the strips into squares of the correct width.

3 Cut the square into two half-square triangles, as above.

4 You can either repeat this procedure on the other diagonal (pic 6) or, if you are wary of the fabric slipping now that it is in two pieces, separate the two triangles and cut them individually. Align one of the horizontal lines of the ruler with the long edge of the triangle, the 45° line with the short edge of the triangle and the edge of the ruler placed on the point of the triangle opposite the long edge. Cut this half-square triangle into two quarter-square triangles.

pic 6

SEAMS

To stitch accurately, you must be able to use the correct seam allowance without having to mark it on the fabric. To do this, you use the foot or the bed of your sewing machine as a guide. Many machines today have a "¼ in" or "patchwork" foot available as an extra. There are also various generic foot accessories available that will fit most machines. Before you start any piecing, check that you can make this seam allowance accurately.

Checking the Machine for the Correct Seam Allowance

Unthread the machine. Place a piece of paper under the presser foot, so that the right-hand edge of the paper aligns with the right-hand edge of the presser foot. Stitch a seam line on the paper. A row of holes will appear. Remove the paper from the machine and measure the distance from the holes to the edge of the paper. If it is not the correct width, i.e. ¼ in/0.75 cm, try one of the following:

1 If your machine has a number of different needle positions, try moving the needle in the direction required to make the seam allowance accurate. Try the test of stitching a row of holes again.

2 Draw a line on the paper to the correct seam allowance,

NOTES

Seams

Unless otherwise stated, the seam allowances are included in the measurements given and are always ¼ in for imperial and 0.75 cm for metric. The metric seam allowance is slightly bigger than the imperial, but it is easy to use in conjunction with the various rotary cutting rulers on the market.

Measurements

The measurements in the quilt instructions are given in both imperial and metric. Use only one set of measurements in any project – do not interchange them, because they are not direct equivalents.

i.e. ¼ in/0.75 cm from the edge of the paper. Place the paper under the presser foot, aligning the drawn line with the needle. Lower the presser foot to hold the paper securely and, to double-check, lower the needle to ensure that it is directly on top of the drawn line.

Fix a piece of masking tape on the bed of the machine so that the left-hand edge of the tape lines up with the right-hand edge of the paper. This can also be done with magnetic strips available on the market to be used as seam guides. But do take advice on using these if your machine is computerized or electronic.

Stitching ¼ in/0.75 cm Seams

When stitching pieces together, line up the edge of the fabric with the right-hand edge of the presser foot or with the left-hand edge of the tape or the magnetic strip on the bed of your machine, if you have used this method.

Checking the Fabric for the Correct Seam Allowance

As so much of the success of a patchwork depends on accuracy of cutting and seaming, it is worth double-checking on the fabric that you are stitching a ¼ in/0.75 cm seam.

Cut three strips of fabric 1½ in/4 cm wide. Stitch these together along the long edges. Press the seams away from the centre strip. Measure the centre strip. It should measure exactly 1 in/2.5 cm wide. If not, reposition the needle/tape and try again.

Stitch Length

The stitch length used is normally 12 stitches to the inch or 5 to the centimetre. If the pieces being stitched together are to be cross-cut into smaller units, it is advisable to slightly shorten the stitch, which will mean the seam is less likely to unravel. It is also good practice to start each new project with a new needle in a clean machine – free of fluff around the bobbin housing.

QUICK MACHINE PIECING

Where you need to stitch together multiple pairs of units as components of repeated blocks, you can speed up the process by a method called chain piecing.

Chain Piecing

Have all the pairs of patches or strips together ready in a pile. Place the first two patches or strips in the machine, right sides together, and stitch them together. Just before reaching the end, stop stitching and pick up the next two patches or strips. Place them on the bed of the machine, so that they just touch the patches under the needle. Stitch off one set and onto the next. Repeat this process until all the pairs are stitched to create a "chain" of pieced patches/strips (pic 7). Cut the thread between each unit to separate them. Open out and press the seams according to the instructions given with each project.

pic 7

PRESSING

Each project will have instructions on the direction in which to press the seam allowances. These have been designed to facilitate easier piecing at junctions and to reduce the bulk so that seam allowances do not lie one on top of the other. Pressing as you complete each stage of the piecing will also improve the accuracy and look of your work. Take care not to distort the patches. Be gentle, not fierce, with the iron.

ADDING THE BORDERS

Most patchwork tops are framed by one or more borders. The simplest way of adding borders is to add strips first to the top and bottom of the quilt and then to the sides, producing abutted corners. A more complicated method is to add strips to adjacent sides and join them with seams at 45 degrees, giving mitred borders. Only the first method is used for the quilts in this book.

Adding Borders with Abutted Corners

The measurements for the borders required for each quilt in the book will be given in the instructions. However, it is always wise to measure your own work to determine the actual measurement.

1 Measure the quilt through the centre across the width edge to edge. Cut the strips for the top and bottom borders to this length by the width specified for the border.

2 Pin the strips to the quilt by pinning first at each end, then in the middle, then evenly spaced along the edge. By pinning in this manner, it is possible to ensure that the quilt "fits" the border. Stitch the border strips into position on the top and bottom edge of the quilt (pic 8). Press the seams towards the border.

pic 8

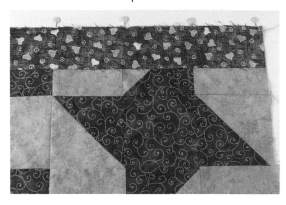

3 Measure the quilt through the centre from top to bottom. Cut the side border strips to this measurement.

4 Pin and stitch the borders to each side of the quilt as before (pic 9). Press the seams towards the border.

pic 9

QUILTING

The three layers or "sandwich" of the backing/wadding/pieced top are held together by quilting or by tying. The quilting can be done by hand or machine. The tying is done by hand stitching decorative ties at strategic points on the quilt. Buttons can also be used for the same purpose but not on quilts for young children.

Layering/Sandwiching

Prior to any quilting, unless you are using a longarm quilting machine, the pieced top must be layered with the wadding and the backing. The wadding and the backing should be slightly larger than the quilt top – approximately 2 in/5 cm on all sides. There are two different methods for assembling the three layers depending on whether the quilts has bound edges or not.

Assembling Prior to Binding

1 Lay out the backing fabric wrong side uppermost. Ensure that it is stretched out and smooth. Secure the edges with masking tape at intervals along the edges to help to hold it in position.

2 Place the wadding on top of the backing fabric. If you need to join two pieces of wadding first, butt the edges and stitch together by hand using a herringbone stitch (pic 10).

pic 10

3 Place the pieced top right side up and centred on top of the wadding.

Assembling Where No Binding is Used – Called "Bagging Out"

1 Spread out the wadding on a flat surface. Smooth out to ensure there are no wrinkles.

2 Place the backing fabric centrally on top of the wadding, right side uppermost.

3 Place the pieced top centrally over the backing, wrong side uppermost. Pin with straight pins around the edges to keep them together.

4 Stitch around all four sides with a $^1/_4$ in/0.75 cm seam allowance but leaving an opening of about 15–18 in/35–45 cm in one of the sides.

5 Trim the excess wadding and backing at the sides and across the corners to reduce bulk, then turn the quilt right side out, so that the wadding is in the middle. Slip-stitch the opening closed.

6 Smooth out the layers of the quilt and roll and finger-press the edges so that the seam lies along the edge or just underneath.

Basting Prior to Quilting

If the piece is to be quilted rather than tied, the three layers now need to be held together at regular intervals. This can be done by basting or by using safety pins. For either method, start in the centre of the quilt and work out to the edges.

Using a long length of thread, start basting in the centre of the quilt top. Only pull about half of the thread through as you start stitching. Once you have reached the edge, go back and thread the other end of the thread and baste to the opposite edge. Repeat this process, stitching in a grid of horizontal and vertical lines over the whole quilt top (pic 11).

pic 11

MACHINE QUILTING

Designs to be used for machine quilting should ideally be those that have one continuous line. The lines can be straight or free-form curves and squiggles. For either type, be sure to keep the density of stitching the same. With either method, continuous lines of stitching will be visible both on the top and on the back of the quilt. It is a quick method but requires careful preparation.

There is a wide variety of tools available designed to help make handling the quilt easier during the machine quilting process. However, the most essential requirement is practice.

It is worth making up a practice sandwich – if possible using the same fabrics and wadding as used in the actual quilt – to be sure that you get the effect you want. In any case, plan the quilting design first, otherwise there is a danger that you will start with quite dense stitching, then tire of the process and begin to space out the lines, producing an uneven pattern.

When starting and stopping the stitching during machine quilting, either reduce the stitch length to zero or stitch several stitches in one spot. If you do not like the build-up of stitches that this method produces, leave long tails on the thread when you start and stop. Later, pull these threads through to one side of the quilt, knot them, then thread them into a needle. Push the needle into the fabric and into the wadding, but not through to the other side of the quilt, and then back out through the fabric again about 1 in/2.5 cm away from where the needle entered the quilt. Cut off the excess thread.

In-the-Ditch Machine Quilting

This is one of the easiest forms of straight line quilting. It involves stitching just beside a seam line on the side without the seam allowances. Some machines require a walking foot to stitch the three layers together. These are used with the feed dogs up and, while in use, the machine controls the direction and stitch length.

Free Motion Machine Quilting

When machine quilting in freehand, a darning foot is used with the feed dogs down, so that you can move the quilt forwards, backwards and sideways. This is easier on some machines than others, but all require a bit of practice.

Hand Quilting

The stitch used is a running stitch and the aim is to have the size of the stitches and spaces between them the same. When the quilt is in the hoop, the surface of the quilt should not be taut, as is the case with embroidery. If you place the quilt top with its hoop on a table, you should be able to push the fabric in the centre of the hoop with your finger and touch the table beneath. Without this "give", you will not be able to "rock" the needle for the quilting stitch. Do not leave the quilt in a hoop when you are not working on it, as the hoop will distort the fabrics.

1 Thread a needle with an 18 in/45 cm length of quilting thread and knot the end. Push the needle into the fabric and into the wadding, but not through to the back, about 1 in/2.5 cm away from where you want to start. Bring the needle up through the fabric at the point where you will begin stitching. Gently pull on the thread to "pop" the knot through into the batting.

2 To make a perfect quilting stitch, the needle needs to enter the fabric perpendicular to the quilt top. Holding the needle between your first finger and thumb, push the needle into the fabric until it hits the thimble on the finger of the hand underneath.

3 The needle can now be held between the thimble on your sewing hand and the thimble on the finger underneath. Release your thumb and first finger hold on the needle. Place your thumb on the quilt top just in front of where the needle will come back up to the top and gently press down on the quilt (pic 12).

pic 12

4 At the same time, rock the thread end of the needle down towards the quilt top and push the needle up from underneath so that the point appears on the top of the quilt. You can either pull the needle through now, making only one stitch, or rock the needle up to the vertical again, push the needle through to the back, then rock the needle up to the quilt top, again placing another stitch on the needle. Repeat until you can no longer rock the needle into a completely upright position (pic 13). Pull the needle through the quilt.

pic 13

5 When the stitching is complete, tie a knot in the thread close to the quilt surface. Push the needle into the quilt top and the wadding next to the knot, but not through to the back of the quilt. Bring the needle up again about 1 in/2.5 cm away and gently tug on the thread to "pop" the knot through the fabric and into the wadding. Cut the thread.

BINDING

Once the quilting is completed, the quilt is usually (but not always) finished off with a binding to enclose the raw edges. This binding can be cut on the straight or on the bias. Either way, the binding is usually best done with a double fold. It can be applied in four separate pieces to each of the four sides, or the binding strips can be joined together and stitched to the quilt in one continuous strip with mitred corners. To join straight-cut pieces for a continuous strip, use straight seams; to join bias-cut pieces, use diagonal seams (pic 14).

pic 14

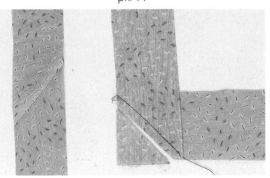

For either method, the width of the bias strips should be cut to the following measurement: finished binding width x four + the seam allowance x two.

For example:

A finished binding width of $\frac{1}{2}$ in would be cut as $2\frac{1}{2}$ in:

$(\frac{1}{2}$ in x 4$) + (\frac{1}{4}$ in x 2$) = 2\frac{1}{2}$ in

or 1.25 cm would be cut 6.5 cm:

$(1.25$ cm x 4$) + (0.75$ cm x 2$) = 6.5$ cm

Binding the Four Sides Separately

1 Cut binding strips to the required width. Fold in half lengthwise with wrong sides together and lightly press.

2 Measure the quilt through the centre from top to bottom and cut two of the binding strips to this length.

3 Pin one of the strips down the side of the quilt, right sides together and aligning raw edges. Stitch with the usual seam allowance.

4 Fold the binding strip to the back of the quilt and slip stitch to the backing fabric. Trim the ends level with the wadding. Do the same on the opposite side of the quilt with the other strip.

5 Measure the quilt through the centre from side to side and add $1\frac{1}{2}$ in/4 cm for turnings. Cut two more binding strips to this length, joining if necessary. Stitch to the top and bottom of the quilt, leaving a $\frac{3}{4}$ in/2 cm overhang at each end. Turn in a short hem at either end before folding to the back and slip-stitching down. Slip stitch the corners neatly.

Continuous Strip Binding

1 Fold the binding in half lengthwise with wrong sides together and lightly press.

2 Place the raw edges of the binding to the raw edge of the quilt – somewhere along one side, not at a corner. Commence stitching about 1 in/2.5 cm from the end of the binding and, using the specified seam allowance, stitch the binding to the quilt through all layers of the "sandwich" (pic 15). Stop $\frac{1}{4}$ in/0.75 cm from the end. At this point, backstitch to secure, then break off the threads. Remove the quilt from the sewing machine.

pic 15

3 Place the quilt on a flat surface, with the binding just stitched at the top edge; fold the binding up and away from the quilt to "twelve o'clock", creating a 45° fold at the corner (pic 16).

pic 16

4 Fold the binding back down to "six o'clock" aligning the raw edges of the binding to the raw edge of the quilt. The fold created on the binding at the top should be the same distance away from the seam as the width of the finished binding (pic 17).

pic 17

5 Start stitching the binding to the quilt at the same point where the previous stitching stopped. Secure with backstitching, then continue to the next corner. Repeat the process at each corner.

6 Stop about 2 in/5 cm from where you started. Open out the fold on both ends of the binding, then seam the two ends together. Trim away the excess, refold and finish applying the binding to the quilt.

7 Trim the excess wadding and backing fabric so that the distance from the stitching line equals or is slightly wider than that of the finished binding. Fold the binding over to the back and hand stitch the folded edge of the binding to the quilt along the row of machine stitching just created. A mitre will appear at the corners on the front and on the back of the binding. Slipstitch these in place (pic 18).

pic 18

Spring Chick Cot Quilt

Designed by **Janet Goddard**

A sunny little cot quilt stitched in fresh spring yellows, greens and white with a cheeky chick appliqué to brighten up any nursery.

Quilt Plan

Finished size: 52 x 39 in/129 x 96 cm

Materials

All fabrics used in the quilt are 45 in/115 cm, 100% cotton.

Background and corner squares: white, 20 in/50 cm
Large triangles and inner border: pale green, 24 in/60 cm
Chick appliqué and sashing: yellow swirl, 20 in/50 cm
Wings: yellow check, 12 in/30 cm square
Beaks: orange, 6 in/15 cm square
Outer border and binding: yellow, 30 in/80 cm
Wadding: 56 x 43 in/139 x 106 cm
Backing: 56 x 43 in/139 x 106 cm in colour of your choice
Embroidery thread: brown embroidery thread
Fusible webbing: 10 in/25 cm
Quilting thread: invisible thread

Alternative Colour Schemes

This quilt is equally effective in alternative pastel colourways. Each of these four blocks
shows the chick in one colour on a white square bordered by a complementary colour.
The quilt could be made in a single colourway or in a combination of two colourways.

1 Blue and yellow is a popular colour combination.

2 Soft pink with a blue check would suit either a baby boy or girl.

3 Green and pink in muted tones is restful.

4 Shades of lilac make a harmonious colour scheme.

Cutting

1 From the white fabric, cut six 7½ in/20 cm squares and 12 x 3½ in/9 cm squares.

2 From the pale green fabric, cut 12 x 6¼ in/17 cm squares. Cross-cut on the diagonal to produce 24 half-square triangles.

3 From the yellow swirl fabric, cut 17 strips, 3½ x 10½ in/9 x 26.5 cm.

Stitching

1 Place a pale green triangle on opposite sides of one of the large white squares, right sides together and aligning the diagonal edge of the triangle with the edge of the square. Pin and stitch, taking a ¼ in/0.75 cm seam allowance **(diagram 1)**. Press the seams towards the triangles. Repeat with the remaining five white squares.

diagram 1

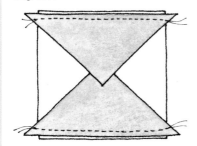

2 Stitch the remaining triangles to the other two sides of the squares in the same way **(diagram 2)**. Press the seams towards the triangles and trim away any over-hanging points.

diagram 2

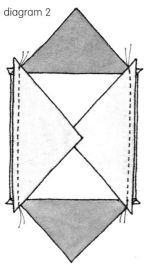

3 Using the chick template above, trace six chick bodies, wings and beaks onto the paper side of the fusible web.

TEMPLATE
Actual size

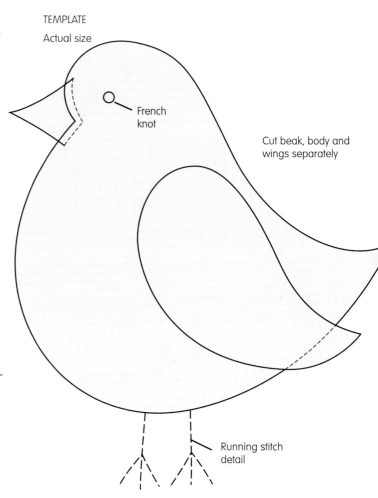

French knot

Cut beak, body and wings separately

Running stitch detail

4 Cut out the shapes. Iron the fusible webbing chick bodies to the reverse of the yellow swirl fabric, the wings to the yellow check fabric, and the beaks to the orange fabric. Cut out carefully.

Note
If you want three chicks to face the opposite direction, reverse the paper templates before tracing onto the fusible web.

5 Remove the backing paper from the shapes and position the beaks and chick bodies onto the squares stitched in steps 1 and 2. Each inner square is on point and the chicks are centred on these. Position the beak first so that the head can be added to cover the raw edge. Press to bond the fabrics to the background. Zig-zag stitch around the shapes, matching the threads to the fabric. Add the wings and zig-zag stitch around these.

6 Using the brown embroidery thread, add legs to the chicks using a running stitch. Stitch a French knot for the eyes (diagram 3).

diagram 3

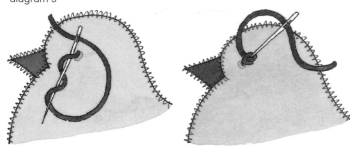

7 Following the quilt plan on page 16, lay out the blocks with the 3½ x 10½ in/9 x 26.5 cm sashing strips of yellow swirl fabric and the 3½ in/9 cm white squares.

8 Pin and stitch the blocks together in horizontal rows with a sashing strip in between and one at either end. Press the seams away from the pale green triangles.

9 Pin and stitch the horizontal sashing strips together with a small white square in between and one at either end. Press the seams away from the small white squares.

10 Pin and stitch the rows together, matching seams carefully, to complete the pieced centre.

Adding the Borders

1 To add the inner border, measure the pieced top through the centre from top to bottom, then cut two strips to this measurement and 2 in/5 cm deep from the pale green fabric. Stitch to the sides of the quilt.

2 Measure the pieced top through the centre from side to side, then cut two strips to this measurement and 2 in/5 cm deep from the pale green fabric. Stitch to the top and bottom of the quilt.

3 To add the outer border, measure again, as above, and cut five strips, 3½ in/9 cm deep, from the yellow fabric. Join three of these strips into one long piece, then cut into two. Stitch the strips to the sides, top and bottom.

Finishing

1 Spread the backing right side down on a flat surface, then smooth out the wadding and the patchwork top, right side up, on the top. Fasten together with safety pins or baste in a grid.

2 Machine quilt with invisible thread. Quilt each block in-the-ditch around the outer white square and the outer green square. Quilt each of the sashing strips and the small white square by stitching ¼ in/0.75 cm inside each seam line (diagram 4). Quilt the green border in-the-ditch on the outer edge.

diagram 4

3 From the remaining yellow fabric, cut five strips of fabric 2 in/5 cm deep, across the width of the fabric. Join three of these into one long piece, then cut into two. Press the strips in half lengthwise, wrong sides together.

4 Pin one strip along one side of the quilt, aligning raw edges. Trim to fit and stitch taking the usual seam allowance, fold to the back of the quilt and hem stitch in place along the stitching line. Repeat on the opposite side.

5 For the top and bottom binding, trim the strips so that they are ¼ in/0.75 cm longer than the quilt at each end. Stitch to the quilt as before but fold in the short overlap first, then fold the binding to the back and hem stitch.

Nursery Windows

Designed by **Dorothy Wood**

A cheerful cot quilt suitable for a baby boy or girl with a novelty print bordered by a triple frame. This is a variation of the traditional "Attic Windows" block: the mitred corners are simply made by using templates.

Quilt Plan

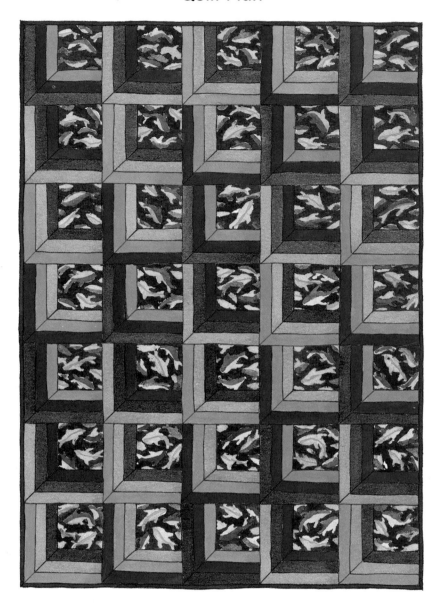

Finished size: 53 x 38 in/131 x 94 cm

Materials

All fabrics used in the quilt are 45 in/115 cm wide, 100% cotton.

Squares: fish print, 30 in/75 cm
Angled strip borders: blue, red, purple and green, 24 in/60 cm of each
Backing: 57 x 42 in/141 x 104 cm in fabric of your choice
Wadding: lightweight, 57 x 42 in/141 x 104 cm
Quilting thread: deep blue
Binding: deep blue, 12 in/30 cm

Alternative Colour Schemes

1 Mix checks, ginghams and plains in primary colours for a bright country style quilt.

2 Use coordinating pastel ginghams and plain fabrics to tone in with a pretty baby print for a soft and restful colourway.

3 Pick bold colours from a pretty baby print fabric to create a striking quilt.

4 This brightly coloured squared print enhances the window effect of this quilt.

Cutting

1   From the fish print fabric, cut five strips, 5 in/12.5 cm deep, across the width, then cross-cut into thirty-five 5 in/12.5 cm squares.

2   Cut each of the four plain fabrics into six 1½ in/4 cm strips. Choosing either the metric or the imperial templates, trace each of the templates below and add a ¼ in/0.75 cm seam allowance all round. Use one of the longest paper templates to cut nine angled pieces from each of the four strips just cut. Repeat with the other templates, until you have nine of each shape, in each colour. Then reverse the templates and repeat.

TEMPLATES at 75% Enlarge on a photocopier by 133%

imperial

metric

Stitching

1   Arrange the border pieces by shape, colour and size on a flat surface. Beginning with the shortest piece of each set, stitch the angled pieces together in sets of three with no two of the same colour in each set (diagram 1). Press all the seams of one set towards the longest strip, and the matching (mirror image) sets towards the shortest strip.

diagram 1

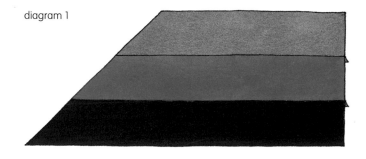

2 Pin and stitch the two sets of matching pieces together along the diagonal to form L-shapes **(diagram 2)**. Press the seams to one side.

diagram 2

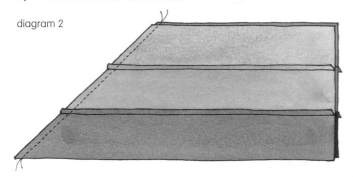

3 Pin the fish print squares into the L-shapes, right sides together and matching the corners carefully. Stitch along one side **(diagram 3)**. Turn the square and fit to the adjacent side and stitch. Press the square's seams outwards.

diagram 3

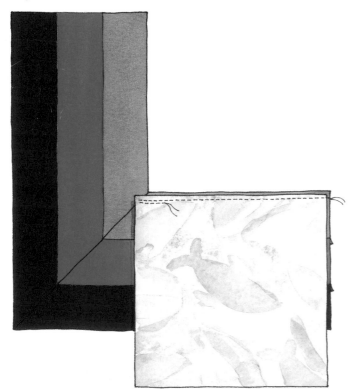

4 Following the quilt plan on page 22 and working from the bottom row, stitch the blocks together to form seven rows of five blocks. On the first, third, fifth and seventh rows press the seams to the left and on the second, fourth and sixth rows, press the seams to the right.

5 Pin the rows together, matching seams. Stitch the rows together. Press the seams flat and press the pieced top carefully.

Finishing

1 Spread the backing right side down on a flat surface, then smooth out the wadding and the quilt top, right side up, on top. Fasten together with safety pins or baste in a grid.

2 Machine quilt in-the-ditch using the deep blue thread. Stitch around the square patches, and then along all the seams except the 45° join between the angled pieces. Take the thread ends through to the reverse of the quilt, tie off and stitch in.

3 Measure the pieced top through the centre from side to side, then cut two binding strips to this measurement and 2 in/5 cm deep. Stitch to the top and bottom of the quilt, taking a ½ in/1.5 cm seam allowance. Fold over to the reverse, turn under a hem and tack in place. Trim the ends level with the wadding.

4 Measure the pieced top through the centre from top to bottom, then cut two more binding strips to this measurement plus 1 in/2.5 cm and 2 in/5 cm deep. Stitch to the sides as before **(diagram 4)**, then turn in the short ends before folding to the back. Pin, tack, then slipstitch the binding to the reverse of the quilt.

diagram 4

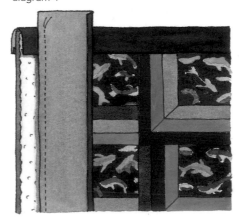

Tic-tac-toe Crib Quilt

Designed by **Alison Wood**

Soft pink and green fabrics combine with a plain ivory fabric background for this new baby's quilt. The piecing has been kept simple: nine-patches alternate with the Shoofly block in a setting known as Tic-tac-toe (a game similar to noughts and crosses). The quilt has been machine-quilted for speed, but would also look wonderful hand-quilted.

Quilt Plan

Finished size: 52 x 40 in/140 x 107 cm
The finished block is 6 in/16.5 cm square

Materials

All fabrics used in the quilt are 45 in/115 cm wide, 100% cotton.

Central blocks: pink and green, 18 in/50 cm of each
For the background and borders: ivory, 2¼ yds/2 m
Backing: 1¾ yds/ 1.5 m in colour of your choice
Binding: pink, 18 in/40 cm
Wadding: 45 x 60 in/115 x 150 cm, cotton or 80:20 cotton/polyester mix for machine quilting. For hand quilting use either cotton/cotton blend or 2 oz polyester.
Medium lead pencil or quilt marking pen
Hera marker and long ruler

Alternative Colour Schemes

1 Amish plains suit this traditional-style quilt.
2 1930s reproduction fabrics in green and yellow make a fresh and pretty quilt.
3 Navy plaids on calico create a country look.
4 Bright novelty prints give a modern twist.

Be wary of using directional or striped fabrics for this quilt, and only choose plaids if you like a relaxed "off-grain" look.

Cutting

1 For the 17 nine-patch blocks, cut four strips of pink fabric and five strips of ivory fabric, each 2½ in/7 cm deep, across the width of the fabric. Cut two strips of pink fabric and three strips of ivory fabric, 2½ in/7 cm deep, across the width and cut these strips in half along the fold of the fabric.

2 For the 18 shoofly blocks, cut two strips of green fabric and four strips of ivory fabric, each 2½ in/7 cm deep, across the width of the fabric. Cut a further three 2½ in/7 cm strips of ivory fabric and cross-cut these into 36 x 2½ in/7 cm squares. Cut three strips of green fabric and three strips of ivory fabric 2⅞ in/8 cm wide and cross-cut these into 36 x 2⅞ in/8 cm squares of each colour to make the 72 half-square triangle units.

3 From the ivory fabric, cut four strips, 5½ in/14 cm deep, across the width, for the borders.

4 From the binding fabric, cut five strips, 2½ in/7 cm deep, across the width of the fabric.

Stitching

1 To make the nine-patch blocks, stitch together one strip of pink fabric between two strips of ivory fabric, and one strip of ivory fabric between two strips of pink fabric, right sides together along the length of the strips. Chain piecing the strips will save time and thread. Press towards the pink fabric.

2 Place one pair of stitched strips on top of the other pair of stitched strips, so that the pink fabric is on top of the ivory and vice versa. The seam allowances should butt together along the length of the strips. Cross-cut the strips into rectangles each 2½ in/7 cm wide (diagram 1). You should be able to cut at least 14 pairs.

diagram 1

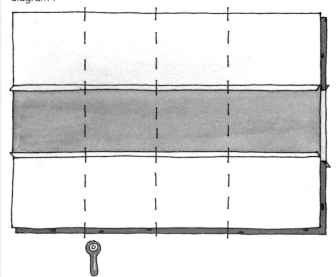

3 Stitch the rectangle pairs together, carefully butting the seam allowances to give well-matched points.

4 Stitch together the remaining full width strip of pink fabric between the two remaining full width strips of ivory fabric, right sides together along the length of the strips. Press as before and cross-cut into rectangles 2½ in/7 cm wide. Stitch to the joined pairs, matching seams, to make 14 nine-patch blocks (diagram 2). Press seam allowances out towards the sides of the blocks.

diagram 2

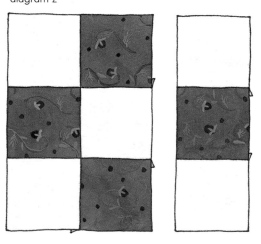

5 Repeat steps 1 to 4 with the half width strips of pink and ivory fabric to make three more nine-patch blocks, giving a total of 17.

6 To make the shoofly blocks, stitch one 2½ in/7 cm strip of green fabric between the two corresponding strips of ivory fabric, right sides together along the length of the strips. Repeat with the remaining 2½ in/7 cm strips of green and ivory fabric. Press towards the ivory fabric. Cross-cut into 18 rectangles each 2½ in/7 cm wide.

7 Draw a diagonal line across the wrong side of each of the 36 ivory 2⅞ in/8 cm squares. Place one green 2⅞ in/ 8 cm square right sides together with one of the marked ivory squares. Stitch a seam line ¼ in/0.75 cm away from, and on each side of, the drawn diagonal line (**diagram 3**). Repeat with the remaining 35 pairs of squares.

diagram 3

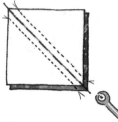

8 Cut the threads between the squares. Press each stitched pair of squares flat to set the seams, then cut along the drawn diagonal line.

9 Press each stitched unit open with the seam allowance towards the green fabric. Trim off the small triangular "ears" to reduce bulk and make it easier to join the units.

10 Join two half-square triangle units with one plain ivory 2½ in/7 cm square in between. Press the seams towards the ivory. Repeat, then stitch together with the rectangles (**diagram 4**). Press the seams towards the middle.

diagram 4

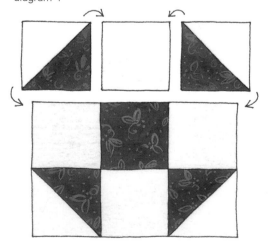

11 Following the quilt plan on page 28, lay out the blocks in seven rows of five blocks alternating the nine-patch and shoofly blocks.

12 Pin and stitch the blocks together into rows. Press the seam allowances between the blocks in opposite directions for alternate rows to butt them together when joining the rows.

13 Pin and stitch the rows together, matching seams carefully, then press the top lightly.

Adding the Borders

1 Measure the pieced top through the centre from top to bottom, then trim two of the 5½ in/14 cm ivory border strips to this measurement. Stitch to the sides, and press.

2 Measure the pieced top through the centre from side to side, then trim the remaining two ivory 5½ in/14 cm borders to this measurement. Stitch to the top and bottom of the quilt, and press.

Finishing

1 Spread the backing right side down on a flat surface, then smooth out the wadding and the patchwork top, right side up, on top. Fasten together with safety pins or baste in a grid.

2 Mark the top with the desired quilting design using a Hera marker and a long ruler. Here, the machine quilting lines run diagonally through the ivory squares and extend out into the borders.

Note
Baste in a grid if planning to hand quilt. If machine quilting, safety pin through all three layers at least every 4 in/10 cm in each direction.

3 Join the binding strips with diagonal seams to make a continuous length to fit all round the quilt and use to bind the edges with a double-fold binding, mitred at the corners.

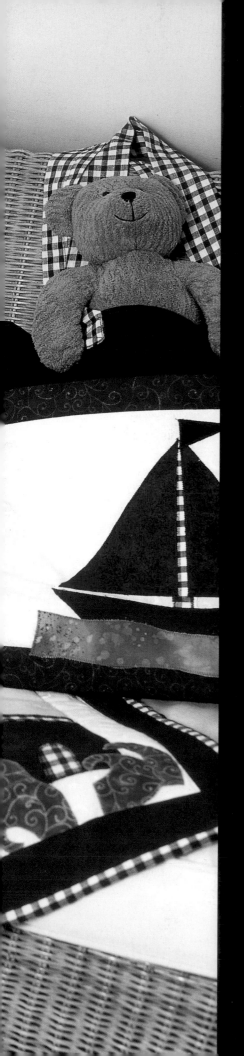

Nautical Playmat with Bag

Designed by **Gail Smith**

I made this playmat quilt for a friend's new baby. It would also be big enough for a cot quilt. I also made a matching bag with pockets on the outside (see page 42). The nautical theme represents all the things we see on a typical summer holiday, and the bright images can be shown to the baby, as he or she gets older. The flag signals spell out "play".

Quilt Plan

Finished size: 47 x 33 in/118.5 x 82.5 cm

Alternative Colour Schemes

Red, white and blue suit the nautical theme best but you could also use other colour combinations as long as the shades are fresh and lively.

1 Yellow, blue and orange make a bright alternative; these fabrics have a weather theme.

2 Introduce checks and woven fabrics for a softer feel or "country" look.

Materials

All fabrics used in the quilt are 45 in/115 cm wide, 100% cotton.

Borders and hull, lighthouse, letters, roof, ball and flags appliqué: red sponge-dyed, 20 in/50 cm

Sashing and appliqué flags, door and lifebelt: navy blue, 10 in/25 cm

Binding and beach hut and lighthouse appliqué: blue gingham, 16 in/40 cm

Background fabric for blocks: white-on-white, 40 in/1 m

Letter and lighthouse: red swirl, 4 in/10 cm

Mast, window and sail border: red gingham, 4 in/10 cm

Numbers and waves: blue swirl, 6 in/15 cm

Sails, number, ball and lighthouse: dark blue sponge-dyed, 6 in/15 cm

Waves and sea: blue watery look, 8 in/20 cm

Ball and clouds: light blue, 8 in/20 cm

Lighthouse, sun, fish, kite and ball: yellow swirl, 6 in/15 cm

Lighthouse, beach, windows and rays of light: yellow sponge-dyed, 4 in/10 cm

Flags and lifebelt: scraps of red, white, yellow and blue fabric

Piping cord: white, 20 in/50 cm

Fusible webbing: 40 in/1 m

Wadding: lightweight, 37 x 51 in/93 x 129 cm

Backing: 40 in/1 m colour of your choice

Coloured threads for embroidery details

Fine black pigma pen (permanent acid-free fine line marker)

Card, for templates

TEMPLATES
All at 50%
Enlarge on a photocopier by 200%

Cutting

1 Cut four 2 in/5 cm strips from the red sponge-dyed border fabric for the borders.

2 From the navy sashing fabric, cut three strips, 1½ in/4 cm deep, across the width of the fabric.

3 From the blue gingham fabric, cut five strips, 1½ in/4 cm deep, across the width of the fabric for the binding.

4 From the white fabric, cut six block backgrounds as follows:
for the ABC block, 39 x 6 in/98.5 x 15 cm;
for the yacht block, 15½ x 14 in/39.5 x 35.5 cm;
for the beach hut block, 15½ x 16 in/39.5 x 41 cm;
for the ball block, 15½ x 13 in/39.5 x 33 cm;
for the flag block, 18½ x 7½ in/47 x 19 cm;
for the lighthouse block, 19½ x 7½ in/49.5 x 19 cm.

5 Enlarge the templates given on pages 36 to 39 to the correct size. Make your own set of templates by glueing the photocopies onto card, then cut out.

6 For the beach and sea, cut a strip, 4 x 15½ in/10 x 39.5 cm, from the blue and from the yellow fabric. Apply fusible webbing to the back of each strip, then cut each in half with a gently curving line. Cut the top edge of the top strip into a similar shape. The bottom edge of the bottom strip can be left straight.

7 Turn each template over and trace the outline of the shapes on to the smooth side of the fusible web. If you do not turn the template over, the final image will be reversed.

8 Cut out the shapes roughly outside the drawn line. Using the materials list and the quilt plan on page 34 for reference, iron the shapes onto the corresponding fabric.

9 Cut out the pieces for each block carefully along the drawn lines and label.

Working the Appliqué

1 Lay out the white fabric background blocks on a table. Arrange each set of appliqué shapes on the corresponding blocks.

2 To position the yacht, take the 15½ x 14 in/39.5 x 35.5 cm block and iron down the mast first, then the sails, sail border, hull, flag and waves. Add the sun shape at the top righthand side (diagram 1).

diagram 1

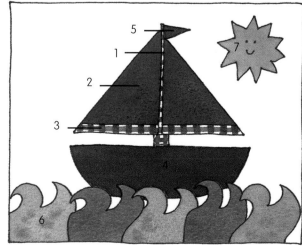

TEMPLATES
All at 50% – enlarge on a photocopier by 200%

NOTE
Some pictures are built up in layers, so you will need to follow the instructions carefully. Don't start stitching until the pieces are ironed in place. When you're happy with the layout, peel off the paper backing and iron each shape into position.

3   To position the beach hut, take the 15½ x 16 in/39.5 x 41 cm block and iron down the beach first, then the sea, hut, windows, doors, roof, lifebelt and kite (**diagram 2**).

diagram 2

4   To position the ball, take the 15½ x 13 in/39.5 x 33 cm block and iron down the beach first, then the sea, light blue ball background, stripes and overlapping clouds. Note that the ball is placed at an angle to give movement to the picture. Position and iron the fish and the top of the ball. **(diagram 3).**

diagram 3

5   Next, iron the flags in position on the 18½ x 7½ in/ 47 x 19 cm block. Following the quilt plan on page 34 for reference, iron down the navy, with white on top; the yellow with navy on top; the white with navy on top; and the yellow with the red on top.

6   Next, iron the lighthouse in place on the 19½ x 7½ in/ 49.5 x 19 cm block. Tuck the top yellow section under the red and iron. Add the blue gingham strip, windows, door, the overlapping waves and the light beams **(diagram 4).**

NOTE
An open zigzag stitch rather than satin stitch is suitable here as you are working with fusible webbing underneath your appliqué shape. Stitch all the pieces of the same colour at the same time, and change the top and bottom threads to match. When you come to an intersection, break the thread, leaving a long end to sew in afterwards, or lockstitch if you have it on your sewing machine.

diagram 4

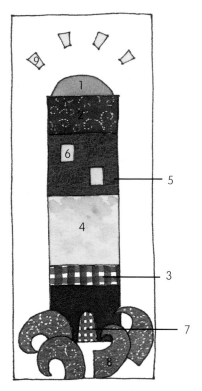

7   Add the numbers 1, 2, 3 and the letters A, B, C evenly spaced and separated by the sun shape to the 39 x 6 in/98.5 x 15 cm block.

Stitching

1   Do a stitch sample on a spare piece of fabric first to work out the best stitch length. Cut a simple shape from spare fusible webbing, iron onto a piece of fabric and cut out. Iron on to a piece of background fabric. Set your machine to a close zigzag stitch and stitch around the edges of the appliqué shape. Adjust the stitch width and length until you are happy, then record the machine settings. Now stitch down all of the appliqué shapes.

2   Straight stitch a blue line from the kite to the edge of the block to make a kite string. Add a length of piping cord down the lefthand side of the flags, aligning with the raw edges of the block at top and bottom.

3   Press all the completed appliqué blocks from the back.

4   Following the quilt plan on page 34, cut two navy sashing strips to fit the top and bottom of the beach hut block and stitch in place. Add the yacht and the ball blocks to the top and bottom. Press the seams towards the darker fabric.

5 Stitch a 2½ x 6 in/6.5 x 15 cm red strip to the top of the ABC block and a 3 x 6 in/8 x 15 cm red strip to the bottom.

6 Stitch a 7 x 7½ in/18 x 19 cm red strip in between the lighthouse and flag block.

7 Lay the middle section between the ABC block and the lighthouse/flag block. Measure the length of these three blocks and trim the remaining navy sashing strips to this measurement (approximately 43½ in/110 cm).

8 Stitch these sashing strips to both sides of the central block, then stitch the ABC block to the left of the central block, and the lighthouse and flag block to the right. Press your work towards the darker fabric.

Adding the Borders

1 Measure the pieced top through the centre from side to side, then trim two of the red sponge-dyed strips to this measurement. Stitch to the top and bottom of the quilt. Press towards the borders.

2 Measure the pieced top through the centre from top to bottom, then trim the remaining two red sponge-dyed strips to this measurement. Stitch to the sides.

Finishing

1 Spread the backing right side down on a flat surface, then smooth out the wadding and the quilt top, right side up, on top. Fasten together with safety pins or baste in a grid.

2 Quilt around the appliqué shapes, about ¼ in/ 0.75 cm outside each shape using white thread. Quilt the same distance inside the straight edges of each block. Stitch a scallop or wave pattern inside the infill blocks.

3 Stitch or draw a smiling face on the suns, if you like.

4 Join the binding strips with diagonal seams to make a continuous length to fit all round the quilt. Use to bind the edges with a double-fold binding, mitred at the corners.

Nautical Quilted Bag

This bag is designed to hold the nautical playmat on page 32. It has a large pocket on the outside to hold items that a mother and baby might need on a trip out.

Materials

All fabrics used for the bag are 45 in/115 cm wide, 100% cotton.

Bag back: 6 in/15 cm navy blue fabric
    4 in/10 cm red swirl fabric
    16 in/40 cm blue gingham
    4 in/10 cm blue swirl fabric
    4 in/10 cm blue water design
    4 in/10 cm red gingham
Background blocks and bag front: 16 in/40 cm white-on-white fabric
Appliqué: Scraps of blue, red and navy fabric
Lining fabric: 20 in/50 cm
Fusible webbing: 10 in/25 cm
Muslin: 18 x 16 in/46 x 41 cm
Wadding: 32 x 47 in/80 x 120 cm
Machine threads to match your fabric
Card, for templates

Cutting

1 Cut a 3$\frac{1}{2}$ x 15$\frac{1}{2}$ in/9 x 40 cm strip from each of the back of the bag fabrics.

2 From the white fabric, cut the following pieces:
14$\frac{1}{2}$ x 10$\frac{1}{2}$ in/37 x 27 cm for the yacht block;
13 x 15 in/33 x 38.5 cm for the pocket lining;
15$\frac{1}{2}$ x 11$\frac{1}{2}$ in/40 x 29.5 cm for the bag front (behind the pocket).

3 From the remaining navy fabric, cut a piece 15$\frac{1}{2}$ x 5$\frac{1}{2}$ in/40 x 14 cm also for the bag front.

4 From the remaining red swirl fabric, cut two strips each 1$\frac{1}{2}$ x 15$\frac{1}{2}$ in/4 x 40 cm for the border.

5 From the remaining navy gingham fabric, cut two pieces for the handles, each
6 x 29$\frac{1}{2}$ in/15 x 75 cm.

6 From the lining fabric, cut one piece 18 x 32 in/46 x 81 cm.

7 For the appliqué, enlarge the relevant templates on page 34 to the correct size. Glue them on to card, then cut out. Also cut a paper strip, 9$\frac{1}{2}$ x 1$\frac{3}{4}$ in/24 x 4 cm, then cut the top and bottom in a gentle curve for the wave template. Turn each piece over, then trace on to the smooth side of the fusible webbing. Cut out roughly. Following the photograph of the finished bag opposite, iron each shape on to the back of the relevant piece of fabric. Cut out on the drawn line. Keep until you are ready to stitch.

8 Cut two pieces of wadding each 15$\frac{1}{2}$ x 16$\frac{1}{2}$ in/40 x 42 cm, and one 15$\frac{1}{2}$ x 12$\frac{1}{2}$ in/40 x 32 cm.

Finished size: $16\frac{1}{2}$ x $14\frac{1}{2}$ in/42 x 37 cm

Stitching

1   To stitch the bag back, first lay out the muslin, with a large piece of wadding on top and fasten with safety pins. Place the red and the blue and white gingham strips at the top, right sides together. Pin and stitch along the lower edge, through all fabrics taking a $\frac{1}{4}$ in/0.75 cm seam **(see diagram 1)**. Open this out, place a pale blue strip over the gingham, right side down and aligning raw edges and stitch along the lower edge as before **(diagram 2)**. Repeat with the remaining three strips, until the whole of the wadding is covered.

diagram 1

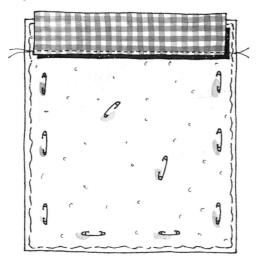

diagram 2

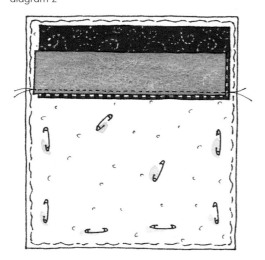

2   To stitch the front pocket, first take the piece of white fabric cut for the yacht block, and stitch the red border strips to all sides. Press towards the darker fabric. Place the appliqué shapes on to the block following the photograph on page 42. Trim a little on all sides to fit the white background, then peel off the paper backing. Iron down the mast into position, then the sails, hull, flag and waves.

3   Stitch the appliqué shapes in position following the tips about the stitching given on page 40.

Finishing

1   Place the blue and white gingham pocket lining piece on top of the pocket, right sides together, then place the small piece of wadding on top. Stitch along the upper edge only. Open out and turn the gingham fabric to the back so that the wadding is sandwiched in between the pocket front and lining. Pin, then quilt round the edge of the block to keep the layers together.

2   Place the $15\frac{1}{2}$ x $5\frac{1}{2}$ in/40 x 14 cm navy piece of fabric at the top of the remaining white piece of fabric, right sides together. Pin and stitch. Press to the darker fabric. Place the remaining wadding underneath. Place the pocket right side up on top of this, forming the bag front and the pocket. Pin and tack **(diagram 3)**.

diagram 3

3 Lay the front and back of the bag on a flat surface, right sides together. Check that they line up correctly, then pin and stitch the sides and bottom, with the usual seam allowance. Check that you stitch through all layers, including the pocket layers. Trim any excess wadding and turn right side out.

4 Fold the lining fabric in half crosswise, right sides together and stitch down the short side adjusting to fit your bag if necessary. Place the lining over the entire bag so the right sides are touching. Pin and stitch round the top of the bag through all layers to attach the lining to the top of the bag.

5 Press 1 in/2.5 cm of the lining to the inside on the bottom edge, and stitch the raw edge to neaten. Pull up the lining, stitch the bottom edges together from the right side **(diagram 4)**, and tuck inside the bag. Topstitch around the top of the bag.

diagram 4

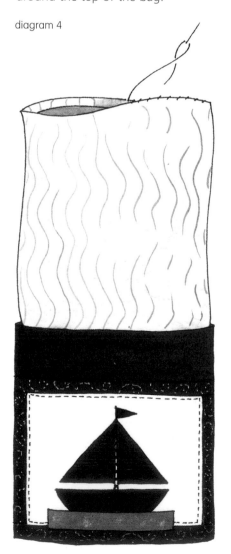

6 To make the navy gingham handles, turn in and press ¼ in/0.75 cm along one long edge. Fold this seam towards the middle and press the other side to the middle, overlapping to seal in the raw edge. The width of the handle should be about 2 in/5 cm. Topstitch along the length of the handles. Turn in 1 in/2.5 cm on the short edge. Press. Pin the handles into position on the outside of the bag. Topstitch with a cross formation **(diagram 5)**.

diagram 5

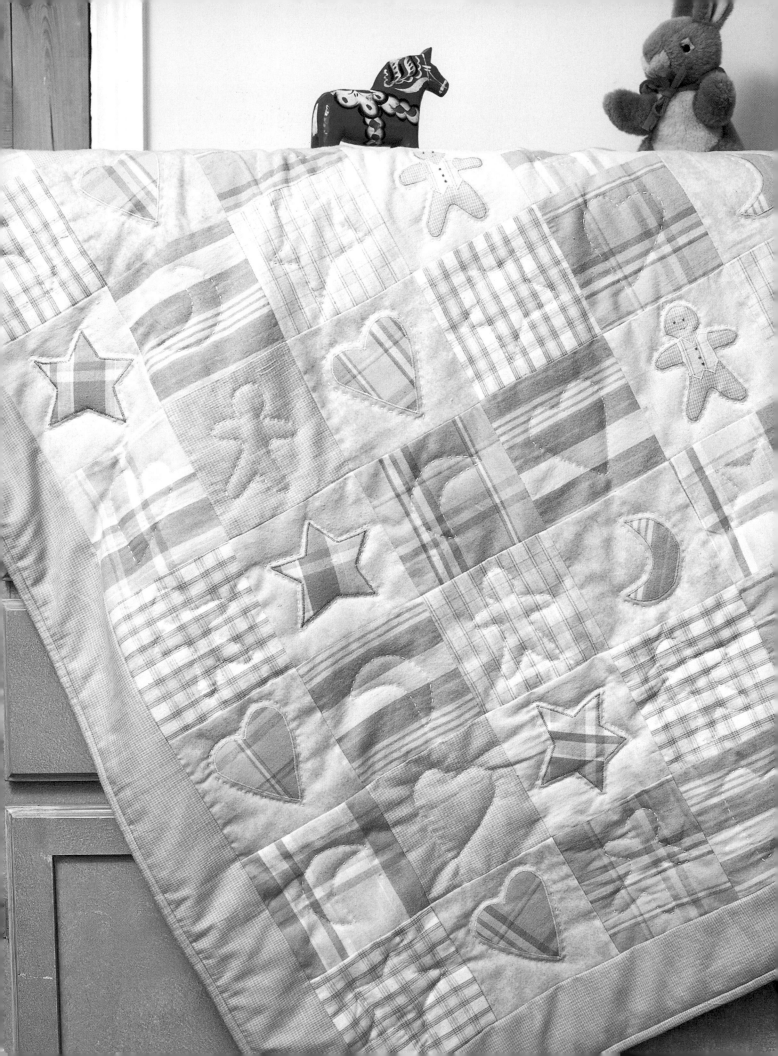

Cookie Cutter Snuggle Quilt

Designed by **Janet Goddard**

A warm snuggle quilt, stitched in soft pastel flannels. The cookie cutter shapes and restful palette of colours evoke the smells of cinnamon baking and the making of cookies.

Quilt Plan

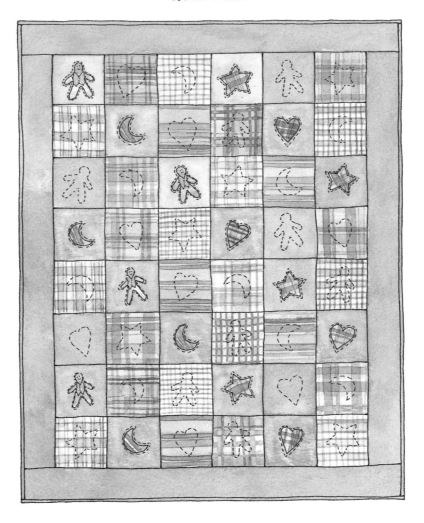

Finished size: 52½ x 41½ in/130 x 103 cm

Materials

All fabrics used in the quilt top are 45 in/115 cm wide, 100% cotton flannel

For the background appliquéd squares: plain cream and plain honey coloured flannel, 15 in/40 cm of each

For the squares and appliqué: six checked and plaid flannel fabrics in soft pastel colours, 10 in/25 cm of each

Template plastic

For the border: small checked flannel, 24 in/60 cm

For the binding: small checked flannel, 12 in/30 cm (this fabric could be the same as the border fabric)

Wadding: lightweight, 57 x 46 in/140 x 113 cm

Backing: flannel fabric, 57 x 46 in/140 x 113 cm in colour of your choice

Fusible webbing: 12 in/30 cm

Embroidery thread: gold embroidery thread for detail on gingerbread men

Quilting thread: beige embroidery thread

Fabric marker

Alternative Colour Schemes

1 A blue and green colour scheme makes a restful quilt for a baby boy.
2 Pick out the colours from this pretty heart fabric for a baby girl's quilt.
3 Have fun with stars and stripes to produce a lively pattern.
4 A mix of pink, blue and yellow makes a sunny design.

Cutting

1 From the plain cream fabric, cut eight 6 in/15 cm squares.

2 From the plain honey coloured fabric, cut eight 6 in/15 cm squares.

3 Label each of the six plaid and checked fabrics with a number from 1 to 6. From each of fabrics 1 and 2, cut six 6 in/15 cm squares.

4 From each of fabrics 3, 4, 5 and 6, cut five 6 in/15 cm squares.

5 From the border fabric, cut five strips, 4½ in/11.5 cm deep, across the width of the fabric.

6 From the binding fabric, cut five strips, 2 in/5 cm deep, across the width of the fabric.

TEMPLATES
Actual size

French
knot detail

running stitch
detail

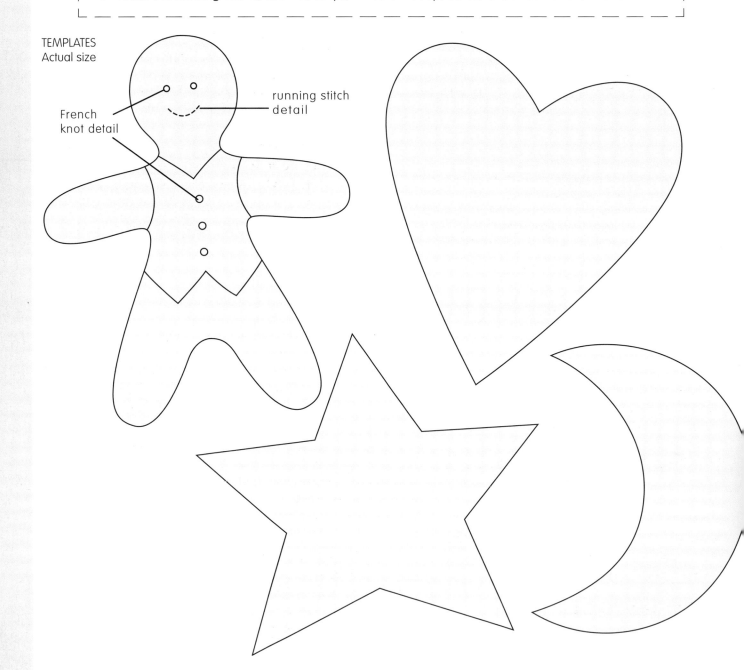

Stitching

1 Using the template plastic, make templates of the gingerbread man, heart, moon and star shapes on page 50. Note that the waistcoats for the gingerbread men must be traced as a separate template.

2 Trace four of each shape (including the waistcoats) onto the paper side of the fusible webbing. Cut out the shapes. Iron the shapes on to the reverse of any of the plaid or checked fabrics that have been left over from cutting the 6 in/15 cm squares. Make sure that you use all fabrics to achieve variety. Cut out carefully.

3 Remove the backing paper from the shapes and position the gingerbread men (without waistcoats) and stars on to the cream fabric squares and the hearts and moons on to the honey coloured squares. Press to bond the fabrics to the background. Zig-zag around the shapes, matching the threads to the fabrics **(diagram 1)**. Add the waistcoats to the gingerbread men and zig-zag around these.

diagram 1

4 Using the gold embroidery thread stitch French knots (see page 19) for the eyes and buttons on the gingerbread men. Add the mouths in running stitch.

5 Following the quilt plan on page 48, lay out the squares in eight rows of six squares.

6 Stitch the squares together in horizontal rows. Press the seams in the first row to the right, then the seams in the second row to the left. Repeat this for all rows. Pin and stitch the rows together. Press.

Adding the Borders

1 Measure the pieced top through the centre from top to bottom, then trim two of the border strips to this measurement. Stitch to the sides of the quilt. If necessary, cut the extra fifth strip in half and stitch one half to two of the border strips to make the required length.

2 Measure the pieced top through the centre from side to side, then the two remaining border strips to this measurement. Stitch to the top and bottom.

Finishing

1 Using the templates of the heart, moon, star and gingerbread man, trace these shapes on to the plain plaid and checked squares in a random manner, one shape to each square.

2 Lay the backing fabric right side down on a flat surface. Lay the wadding and quilt top, right side up on the backing. Pin in place, making sure that all the creases are smoothed out. Tack the layers together, starting in the centre working out towards the borders.

3 Using the beige embroidery thread and a large running type stitch, outline quilt around each appliquéd shape **(diagram 2)** and quilt on the randomly marked shapes **(diagram 3)**.

diagram 2   diagram 3

4 Cut one of the binding strips in half and stitch one half to two of the remaining strips. Press all the strips in half, right sides facing outwards along the length of the fabric.

5 Pin one of the longer binding strips along one side of the quilt, aligning raw edges. Trim to fit and stitch taking the usual seam allowance. Fold to the back and hem stitch in place along the stitching line. Repeat on the opposite side.

6 For the top and bottom, stitch the two shorter strips to the quilt in the same way but before folding to the back, trim the strips so that they are ¼ in/0.75 cm longer than the quilt at each end. Fold in the short overlap, then fold the binding to the back and hem stitch in place.

Special Edition

Designed by **Rosemary Wilkinson**

This little cot quilt is based on the traditional "Postage Stamp" design and the name refers to commemorative issues of stamps for special occasions. It's made from five co-ordinating fabrics and all done with strip piecing.

Quilt Plan

Finished size: 55 x 41 in/140 x 105 cm
Finished size of square: 2¾ in/7 cm

Materials

All fabrics used in the quilt are 45 in/115 cm wide, 100% cotton.

For the pieced top: five soft pastel print fabrics in pink, blue, green and white, 24 in/60 cm of each
Wadding: lightweight, 45 x 60 in/115 x 150 cm
Backing: 45 x 60 in/115 x 150 cm in colour of your choice
Ric-rac braid: cream, 5½ yds/5.10 m
Quilting thread

Alternative Colour Schemes

1 A mix of floral fabrics produces a pretty colour scheme for a baby girl.

2 Bright primaries make a vibrant, cheerful quilt.

3 Try a selection of prints in tones of the same colour for a restful scheme.

4 A jumble of yellows and blues makes a lovely quilt for a baby boy.

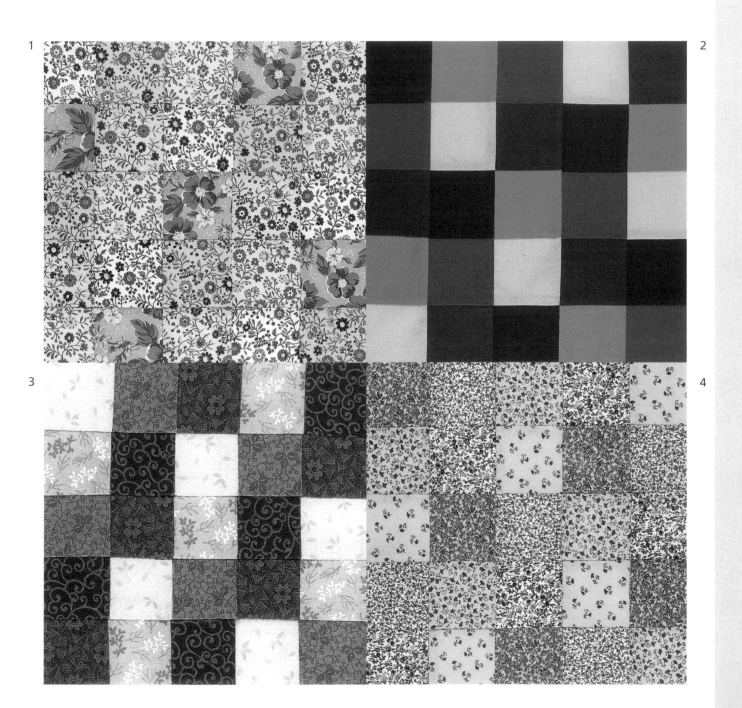

Cutting

1 From each of the soft pastel fabrics, cut six strips, 3¼ in/8.5 cm deep, across the width of the fabric.

Stitching

1 Take one strip of each colour and lay out in your chosen order, then repeat this order twice more, so that you have 15 strips in all (diagram 1).

diagram 1

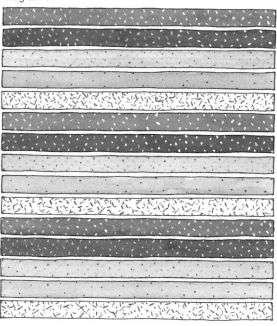

2 Stitch the strips together along the long edges, taking a ¼ in/0.75 cm seam allowance. Repeat to make a second block of 15 strips.

3 Cross-cut 12 vertical strips, 3¼ in/8.5 cm wide from one block and another 8 vertical strips from the second.

4 Take two of these strips and position as horizontal strips on your work surface. Where there are two squares of the same colour touching, unpick the seam and rearrange the sequence of the squares: you may need to do this in two or more places (diagram 2).

diagram 2

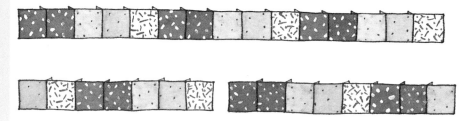

5 Restitch the short seams in the second strip, then pin and stitch these two strips together along the long edges, taking the usual seam allowance and being very careful to match the seams.

6 Place a third strip in position at the bottom of this two-strip unit. Where two squares of the same colour are touching, unpick the seams and rearrange the squares as before, then pin and stitch to the first two strips as before. Repeat until all 20 strips have been joined and no two squares of the same colour are touching anywhere on the pieced top.

7 Place a round object, such as a saucer at each corner and draw around it to round off the corners (diagram 3). Cut around the drawn lines.

diagram 3

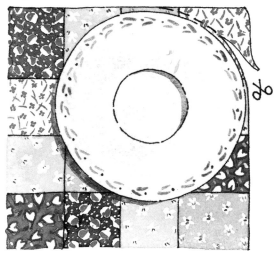

8 Place the ric-rac braid on the edge of the right side of the pieced top, so that the centre of the braid is lying $^1/_4$ in/0.75 cm from the edge. Begin stitching the braid to the quilt about 1 in/2.5 cm from the start of the braid and stitching through the centre of the braid. Stitch the braid all round the edge of the quilt. Where the braid overlaps with the start, turn both ends away from the pieced top and stitch over the join (**diagram 4**).

diagram 4

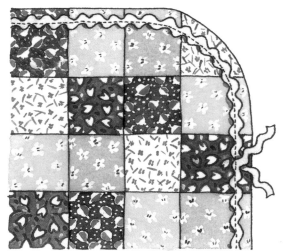

Finishing

1 Smooth out the wadding on a flat surface, then spread the backing on top, right side up. Place the pieced top over the backing, right side down.

2 Pin the sandwich together around the edges, making sure there are no wrinkles in any of the layers.

3 Stitch the three layers together exactly along the stitching line of the ric-rac braid. Stitch around all four sides but leave a 10 in/25 cm gap in one side.

4 Trim the excess wadding back to the seam line, then trim the excess backing to within $^1/_4$ in/0.75 cm of the seam line.

5 Turn the quilt right side out through the gap, so that the wadding is sandwiched between the backing and the pieced top. Roll the edge of the quilt between your fingers to pull out the ric-rac braid, so that it forms an edge to the quilt. Tack around the edge of the quilt just inside the braid.

6 Fasten the quilt layers together with safety pins or baste in a grid.

7 Machine quilt in rectangles between the squares, then stitch all round the edges just inside the edge to hold the ric-rac in place. Remove the tacking threads.

Jungle Playmat

Designed by Gail Smith

There is always a lot going on in the jungle and there is a lot for baby to do with this playmat. It's bright, colourful and comfortable to lie on, and has crackly leaves, furry paw prints and textured features on the snake and lion. The quilting in the border is done using your baby's hands and footprints as templates, creating a permanent reminder of how small he or she once was.

Quilt Plan

Finished size: 37 x 32 in/90 x 78 cm

Materials

All fabrics used in the quilt are 45 in/115 cm wide.

Central blocks: 6 in/15 cm of each of two cotton fabrics – lime green and yellow, and 9 in/23 cm of each of two cotton fabrics – blue print and green daisy

Border: sponge-dyed blue cotton, 16 in/40 cm

Binding: striped cotton, 12 in/31 cm

Leaves: dark green cotton, 6 in/15 cm

Snake: bright green cotton, 6 in/15 cm and 1 yd/1 m yellow ric rac braid

Crackly leaves: space blanket fabric, 10 in/25 cm square and lightweight Interfacing, 10 in/25 cm

Tree trunks and pads: scraps light brown cotton

Paw prints: brown or fawn washable velvet, 10 in/25 cm square

Lion: scraps mustard and yellow cotton, and 8 in/20cm cord for a tail (optional)

Indelible marking pen

Fusible web: 20 in/50 cm

Template paper

Wadding: cotton, 35 x 40 in/86 x 98 cm

Backing: cotton, 1¼ yds/1 m in colour of your choice

Quilting thread: for the baby hands and feet detail

Alternative Colour Schemes

1 Frogs and bug prints in reds, blues and greens make a lively back garden jungle quilt.

2 Turquoise and pink add an element of fantasy.

3 Greens and blues suggest dense foliage and forest pools.

4 Bright oranges and greens make a more exotic looking jungle.

Cutting

1 From the four fabrics for the central blocks, cut the lime green and yellow into two strips, 3 in/7.5 cm deep, across the width of the fabric and cut three strips to the same depth from the blue patterned and the green daisy fabrics.

2 From the blue border fabric, cut four strips, each 4 in/10 cm deep, across the width of the fabric.

3 From the striped binding fabric, cut four strips, 2½ in/6.5 cm deep, across the width of the fabric.

4 For the appliqué shapes (lion, paw prints, tree trunk and snake) photocopy the templates on pages 64 to 65 to the correct size. Glue on to card, then cut out to make templates. Turn each piece over so that it is the reverse side of the shape, then trace on to the smooth side of the fusible web. Cut out roughly. Place rough side down on to the back of the relevant piece of fabric and iron in place. Cut out along the drawn line.

5 For the crackly leaves, make templates as above. Cut the green fabric in half. Draw around the templates to make four of one shape and three of the other on one half of the fabric, leaving at least ½ in/1 cm between each leaf (see also diagram 2). Do not cut out at this stage.

Stitching

1 Pair up the 3 in/7.5 cm strips for the blocks in the following order: lime green and green daisy, blue and green daisy, yellow and blue, lime green and blue, yellow and green daisy. Pin and stitch each pair together down one long side, taking a ¼ in/0.75 cm seam allowance. Press the seams towards the darker fabric.

2 Lay the strips on a cutting board and cross-cut each into 5½ in/13.5 cm sections (**diagram 1**). Press.

diagram 1

3 Following the quilt plan on page 60, lay out the blocks in your chosen colour arrangement in six rows of five blocks each.

4 Stitch the blocks in each row together, taking the usual seam allowance. Press the seams in alternate directions for each row.

NOTE
Pin or tape an identifying letter or number to each row to help you keep the rows in sequence.

5 Pin and stitch the rows together, taking care to line up the seams.

6 Measure the pieced top through the centre from side to side, then trim two of the border strips to this measurement. Stitch to the top and bottom of the quilt.

7 Measure the pieced top through the centre from top to bottom, then trim the remaining two border strips to this measurement. Stitch to the sides.

Working the Appliqué

1   Now you are ready to start the appliqué. Do a stitch sample on a spare piece of fabric first to work out the best stitch length. Cut a simple shape from some spare fusible webbing, iron onto a piece of fabric and cut out. Iron on to a piece of background fabric. Set your machine to a close zigzag stitch and stitch around the edges of the appliqué shape. Adjust the stitch width and length until you are happy with it, then make a note of your machine settings, so you can take a break during stitching.

NOTE

An open zigzag stitch rather than satin stitch is suitable here as you are working with fusible webbing underneath your appliqué shape. Stitch all the pieces of the same colour at the same time, and change the top and bottom threads to match. When you come to an intersection, break the thread, leaving a long end to sew in afterwards, or lockstitch.

2   To stitch the lion, place the lion's body and mane in position following the quilt plan on page 60. Make a knot in one end of the cord for the lion's tail, then place the other end under the fabric, iron, and stitch in place securely. If the mat is for a very young child, you could use a machine satin stitch to make the tail, rather than adding a cord, which could be pulled off. Add the face piece on top of the mane and iron. Stitch all pieces to secure, then draw on the face and mark out the legs.

3   To stitch the snake, first stitch the ric-rac onto the snake, then place the snake in position, iron and stitch.

4   To make the crackly leaves, iron the second piece of green fabric and place right side down. Add a layer of

space blanket fabric, then a layer of interfacing, followed by another layer of space blanket. Finally, add the green fabric onto which you drew the leaves. Pin and tack the layers. With matching thread, stitch around each leaf with a close zigzag stitch (diagram 2). Cut out carefully to avoid cutting the stitching. Reserve until later.

diagram 2

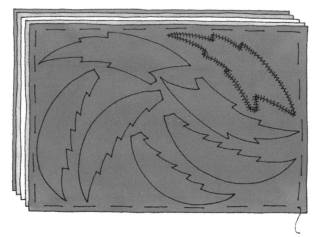

5   Iron and stitch the tree trunk and paws in position.

Finishing

1   Spread the backing right side down on a flat surface, then smooth out the wadding and the quilt top, right side up, on top. Fasten together with safety pins or baste in a grid.

2   Quilt a zigzag pattern across the blocks and make a scallop or wave pattern on the upper and lower borders. To further secure the layers, add detail quilting to the lion's legs and tree trunk.

3   Place the crinkly leaves on the quilt and stitch in position through all the layers with a running stitch down the centre of each leaf. Make your stitching look like leaf veins, if possible. Make sure that they are securely stitched and cannot be pulled off.

4   Draw around the baby's hands and feet and use to make a card template. Alternatively use the templates given on page 65. Trace on to the quilt border at least $\frac{1}{2}$ in/1.5 cm from the edge. Hand quilt around the outlines using a thick thread.

5   Join the binding strips with diagonal seams to make a continuous length to fit all around the quilt. Use to bind the edges with a double-fold binding, mitred at the corners.

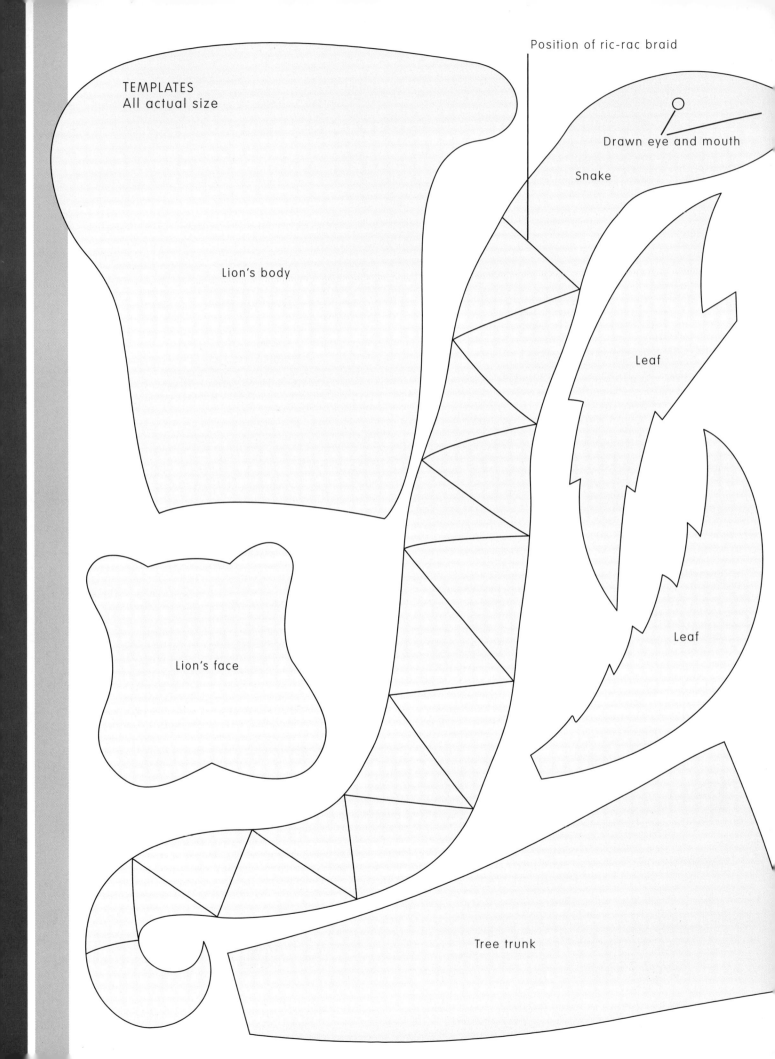

Position of ric-rac braid

TEMPLATES
All actual size

Drawn eye and mouth

Snake

Lion's body

Leaf

Lion's face

Leaf

Tree trunk

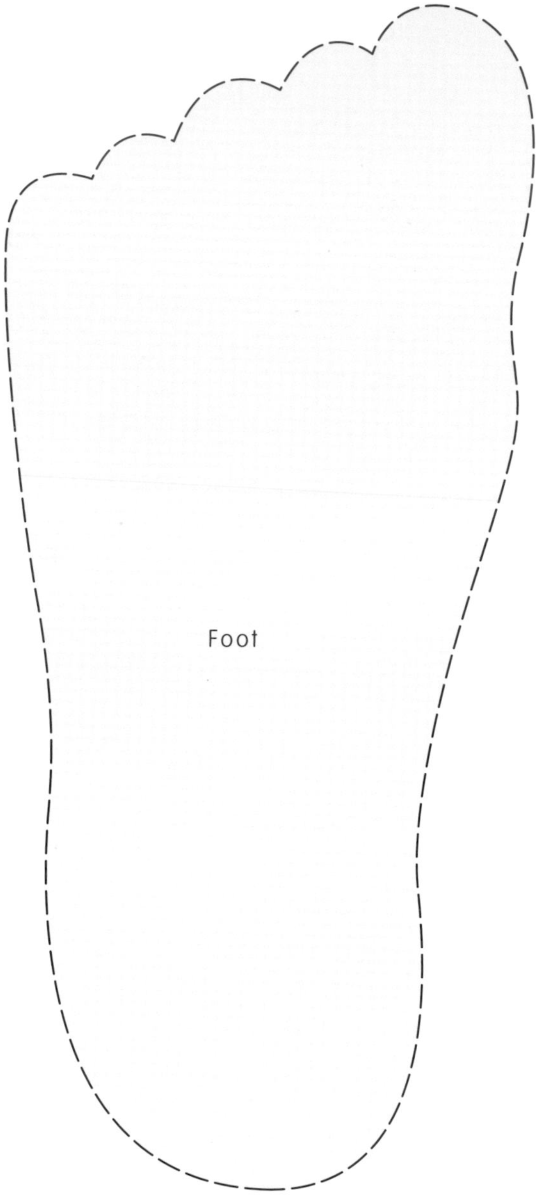

Foot

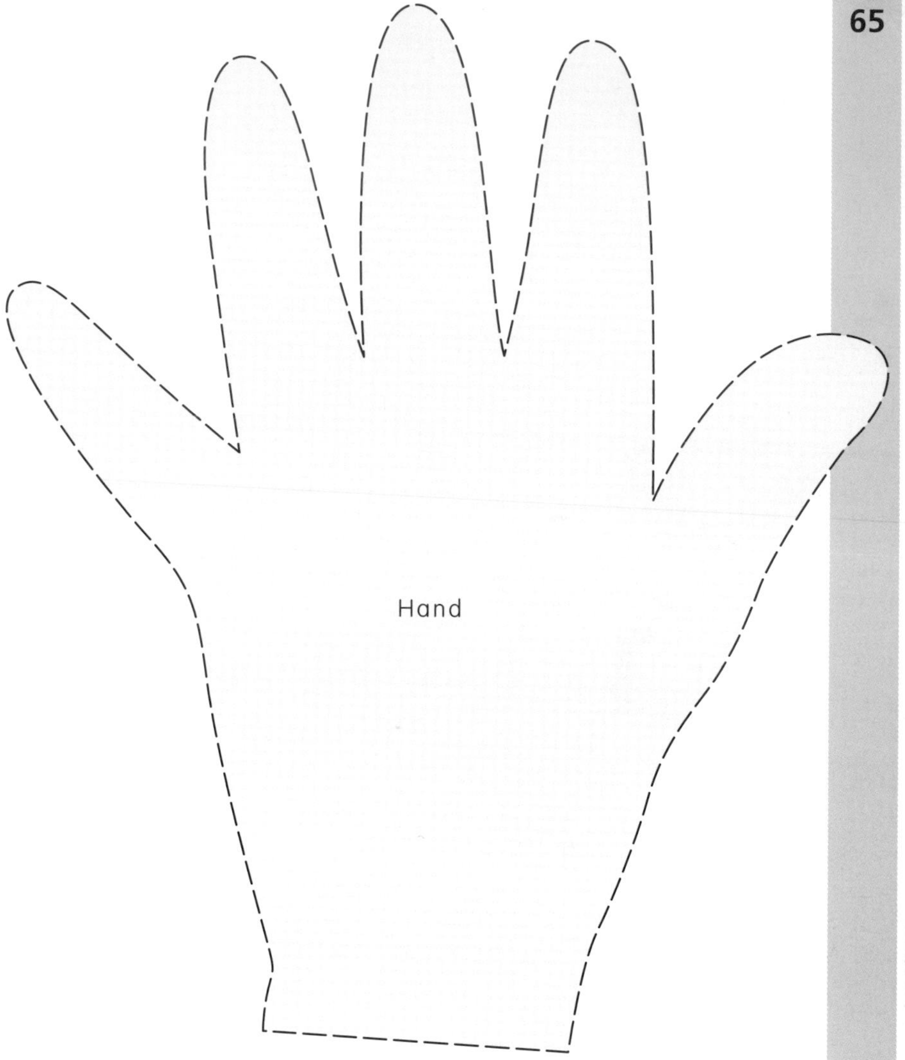

Hand

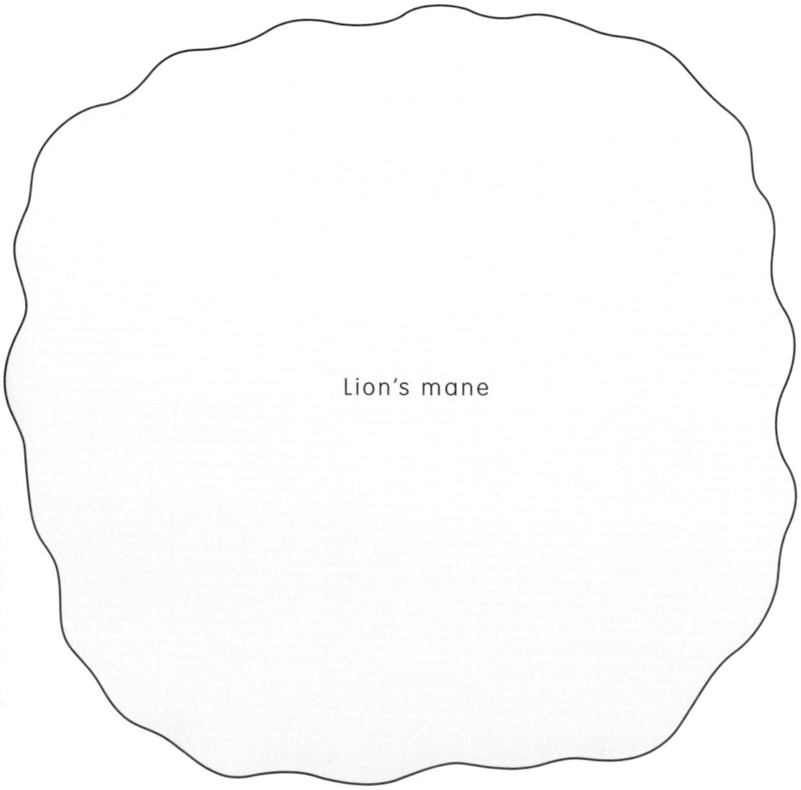

Paws

Lion's mane

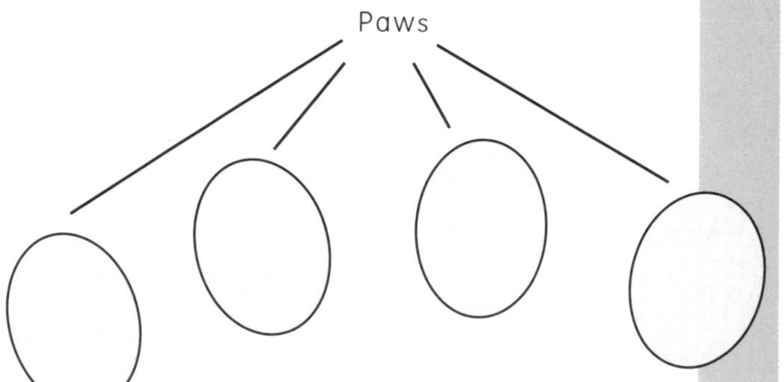

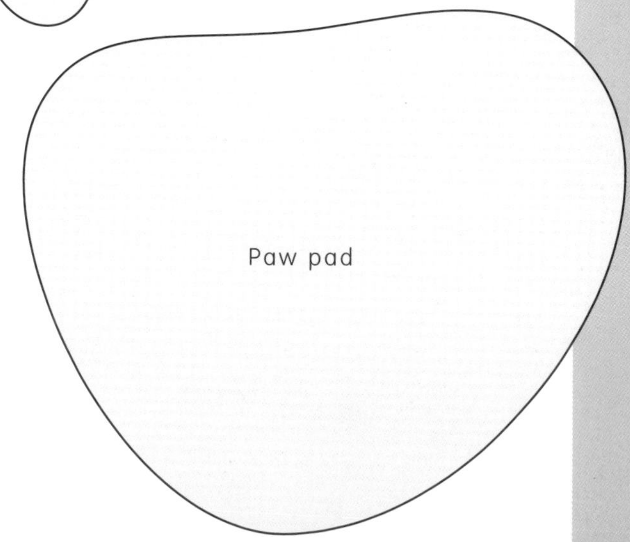

Paw pad

Spinners

Designed by Mary O'Riordan

This snuggle quilt is very easy and quick to make, as the blocks only require squares rotary cut in two different sizes. This is an ideal project for using up lots of little scraps of fabric.

Quilt Plan

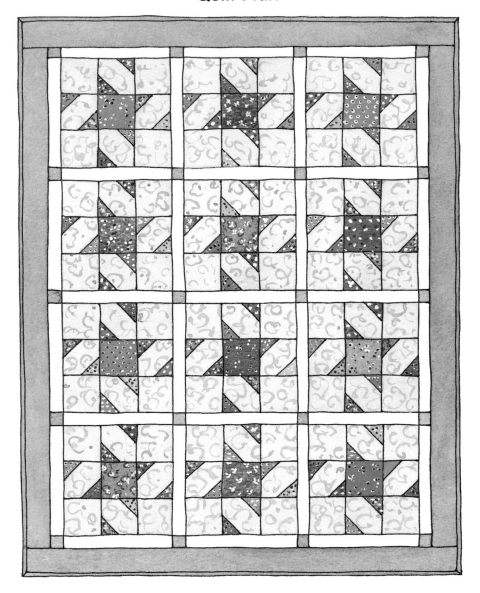

Finished size: 45$\frac{1}{2}$ x 35$\frac{1}{2}$ in/116 x 90.5 cm
Each block is 9 in/23 cm.

Materials

All fabrics in the quilt top are 45 in/115cm wide, 100% cotton.

Spinner fabrics: scraps of bright 1930s reproduction fabrics to total 20 in/50 cm; the minimum size needed is a 3$\frac{1}{2}$ in/9.5 cm square
Background fabric: pale yellow print, 1 yd/1 m
Sashing: white, 14 in/35 cm
Borders, binding and sashing posts: bubblegum pink, 24 in/60 cm
Wadding: lightweight, 40 x 50 in/103 x 130 cm
Backing: 50 in/1.3 m in colour of your choice

Alternative Colour Schemes

1 For a Shaker-style quilt, cut angels and hearts or other favourite motifs from novelty fabrics and use for the centre and corner squares.

2 Combining spots and dots with bright colours is a winning combination for a toddler's quilt.

3 Select fabrics with a celestial theme to echo the spinning stars theme.

4 If making a quilt for a winter baby, choose a fabric to match the season. A red print is perfect for him or her to snuggle under.

Cutting

1 From the spinner fabrics, cut 12 squares, each 3½ in/9.5 cm. Cut the remainder of the spinner fabrics into strips, 2 in/5 cm deep across the width of the fabric and cross-cut to make 96 squares, each 2 in/5 cm square. Alternatively, individually cut the squares from scrap fabrics.

2 From the background fabric, cut eight strips, 3½ in/9.5 cm deep, across the width of the fabric. Cross-cut into 96 squares, each 3½ in/9.5 cm square.

3 From the sashing material, cut eight strips, 1½ in/4 cm deep, across the width of the fabric. Cross-cut into 31 rectangles, 1½ x 9½ in/4 x 24 cm.

4 From the border fabric, cut two strips 2½ x 41½ in/6.5 x 106 cm and two further strips 2½ x 35½ in/6.5 x 90.5 cm. For the sashing posts, cut one strip, 1½ in/4 cm deep across the width of the fabric and cross-cut to produce 20 squares. Cut four strips, 2 in/5 cm deep across the width for the binding.

Stitching

1 Mark a diagonal line on the reverse of eight of the 2 in/5 cm spinner squares. Place two spinner squares on opposite corners of four background squares, right sides together.

2 Stitch along the marked line, then trim ¼ in/0.75 cm from the stitching line **(diagram 1)**. Press the seam allowance towards the spinner triangles.

diagram 1

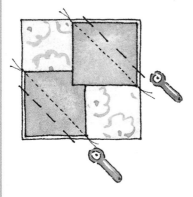

3 Arrange the pieced units with four background squares and one 3½ in/9.5 cm spinner square **(diagram 2)**. Pin and stitch together with an accurate ¼ in/0.75cm seam allowance. Press towards the darker fabric. Repeat to make a total of 12 blocks in the same way.

diagram 2

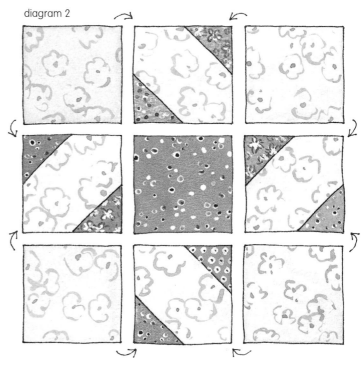

4 Following the quilt plan on page 68, stitch four rows of three blocks together with a white sashing strip between each block and at the beginning and end of each row.

5 Stitch five rows of sashing posts and sashing strips together, beginning and ending with a pink sashing post and with three sashing strips per row (**diagram 3**).

diagram 3

6 Pin and stitch the rows together with a strip of sashing between each row and at the top and bottom of the pieced centre.

Adding the Borders

1 Stitch the 2½ x 41½ in/6.5 x 105 cm border strips to the sides of the quilt, taking a ¼ in/0.75 cm seam allowance. Stitch the two remaining border strips to the top and bottom taking the usual seam allowance. Press the seams towards the borders.

Finishing

1 Spread the backing right side down on a flat surface, then smooth out the wadding and the patchwork top, right side up, on top. Fasten together with safety pins or baste in a grid.

2 Quilt in-the-ditch along the sashing lines and quilt two parallel lines diagonally in both directions through the centre of each block (**diagram 4**).

diagram 4

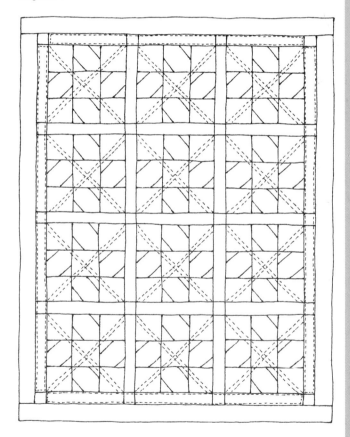

3 Join the binding strips with diagonal seams to make a continuous length to fit all round the quilt and use to bind the edges with a double-fold binding, mitred at the corners.

Fairy Princess

Designed by **Sarah Wellfair**

This is a simple two-block quilt using a four-patch and snowball block, which together create stars out of the four-patch. The pink, yellow and blue solids pick out the colours in the fairy print fabric, making a really magical quilt for a little girl. It has a soft, warm, fleece backing, so no wadding is required.

Quilt Plan

Finished size: 53 x 45 in/131 x 111 cm
Finished block size: 4 in/10 cm

Materials

All fabrics used in the quilt are 45 in/115 m wide, 100% cotton.

For the four-patch blocks: solid pink and heart print, 18 in/40 cm of each
For the snowball blocks centres and outer borders: fairy print, 1⅔ yds/1.5 m
For the snowball block corners: yellow, 30 in/75 cm
Binding: pink, 20 in/ 50 cm
Backing: fleece, 56 x 48 in/140 x 120 cm in colour of your choice
Inner borders: blue, 16 in/40 cm

Alternative Colour Schemes

1 Spots and stripes reduce the star effect. The bold spot fabric is very dominant, making the four-patch the major pattern.

2 Frogs and bugs are a great alternative for little boys. Using two colours creates a different pattern.

3 Hats and feathers are fun for little girls: the soft floral and feather fabrics make the red stars very bold.

4 Self-patterned bright fabrics are good for boys and girls of all ages.

Cutting

1 From each of the solid pink and heart print fabrics, cut five strips, $2\frac{1}{2}$ in/6.5 cm deep, across the width of the fabric.

2 From the fairy print fabric, cut four strips, 4 in/10 cm wide, down the length of the fabric. Cut four strips, $4\frac{1}{2}$ in/11.5 cm wide, down the length, then cross-cut these strips into 40 x $4\frac{1}{2}$ in/11 cm squares.

3 From the yellow fabric, cut nine strips, $2\frac{1}{4}$ in/6 cm deep, across the width of the fabric. Cross-cut these strips into 160 x $2\frac{1}{4}$ in/6 cm squares. On the back of each cream square, draw a pencil line from corner to corner on the diagonal.

4 From the binding fabric, cut five strips, 3 in/8 cm deep, across the width of the fabric.

Stitching

1 To make the four-patch block, take one strip of pink and one of heart print fabric and place right sides together. Stitch down the length, taking a $\frac{1}{4}$ in/0.75 cm seam allowance. Repeat with the remaining four strips of each shade. Press the seams towards the solid pink. Cross-cut into $2\frac{1}{2}$ in/6.5 cm units to make 80 strips (diagram 1).

diagram 1

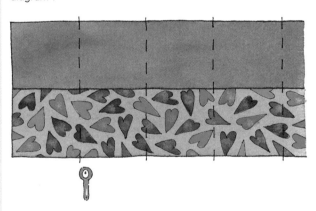

2 Take two cross-cut units, turn one upside down, then pin and stitch right sides together to make a four-patch block (diagram 2). Repeat until you have 40 four-patch blocks.

diagram 2

3 To make the snowball block, place one yellow square on the corner of each fairy square, right sides together. Stitch along the marked pencil line (diagram 3). Repeat for all 40 squares.

diagram 3

4 Take a second square and place on the opposite corner of each square. Stitch in the same way. Stitch the remaining squares to the remaining corners in the same way.

5 Trim all four corners $\frac{1}{4}$ in/0.75 cm from the seam (diagram 4). Press the corners out towards the cream to complete the snowball block (diagram 5). You should now have 40 snowball blocks and 40 four-patch blocks.

diagram 4   diagram 5

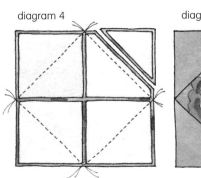

6 Following the quilt plan on page 74, lay out the blocks in ten rows of eight blocks, alternating the four-patch and snowball blocks. Pin and stitch the blocks together in rows, then pin and stitch the rows together, being careful to match the seams.

Adding the Borders

1 For the inner borders, measure the pieced top through the centre from side to side, then cut two strips to this measurement and 4½ in/11.5 cm deep from the blue fabric, joined as necessary. Stitch to the top and bottom of the quilt.

2 Measure the pieced top through the centre from top to bottom, then cut two strips to this measurement, 4½ in/11 cm deep, from the remaining blue fabric, joined as necessary. Stitch to the sides.

3 For the outer borders, repeat steps 1 and 2 using the four fairy print border strips, trimmed as necessary.

Finishing

1 Spread the backing right side down on a flat surface, then smooth out the patchwork top, right side up, on top. Fasten together with safety pins or baste in a grid.

2 Quilt in-the-ditch between the blocks, or quilt as desired. Trim the backing to the edge of the quilt.

3 Join the binding strips into one long length, then fold in half down the length, wrong sides together, and press.

4 Measure across the quilt in the centre from side to side and cut two binding strips to this size. Stitch to the top and bottom of quilt, matching the raw edges. Stitch to the back of the quilt, not the front, as this will make it easier to slip stitch down. Slip stitch in place on the front.

5 Measure the quilt across the centre from top to bottom. Add ¼ in/0.75 cm to either end and cut two bindings to this measurement, joining the pieces as necessary. Stitch in the same way as before, leaving the usual seam allowance at each end. Turn in the ends and flip the binding to the front of the quilt, and stitch down.

Triangular Playmat

Designed by **Dorothy Wood**

Have fun with these triangle blocks to create an eye-catching playmat for a young baby.

Quilt Plan

front

back

Finished size: 36 x 36 in/108 x 108 cm (at widest points)

Materials

All fabrics used in the quilt are 45 in/115 cm wide, 100% cotton.

Small triangles: cat print, one fat quarter (18 x 21 in/50 x 52 cm)
Angled border pieces and backing triangles: blue, green and red plain fabric,
20 in/50 cm of each plus a 9 x 21 in/25 x 53 cm piece of pale blue
Wadding: lightweight, 38 x 38 in/113 x 113 cm
Machine thread to match your fabrics
Tapestry needle

Alternative Colour Schemes

1 Pick out two toning colours from a simple print fabric to create an appealing heart motif quilt.

2 Make a multicoloured, abstract look less busy by bordering each triangle with a single colour and using a range of plain colours to complete the quilt.

3 Classic white daisies with blue and white patches are enhanced with a yellow border.

4 Pastel ginghams often look lighter than plains; team them with a fun baby print for a really fresh look.

Cutting

1 From each of the green, red and blue fabrics, cut one strip, $3\frac{1}{2}$ in/9.5 cm deep, across the width of the fabric for the borders.

2 Enlarge and cut out the large triangle template opposite in paper. Place the template on one of the backing triangle fabrics and, adding a $\frac{1}{4}$ in/0.75 cm seam allowance, cut out one large triangle. Repeat with each backing colour to make four large triangles from each.

3 Enlarge and cut out the small triangle from the same template. Pin the template to the cat print fabric with the triangle pointing upwards. Add a $\frac{1}{4}$ in/0.75 cm seam allowance all round, and cut out. Using the template, cut a further nine triangles pointing upwards, then reposition the template on the fabric and cut out six more triangles pointing downwards.

4 Enlarge and cut out the two angled strips from the same template. From the blue fabric, use the templates to cut out six short strips and five long strips, adding the usual seam allowances. From the green fabric, cut five strips of each size, and from the red fabric, cut five short strips and six long strips.

Stitching

1 Following the plan of the front of the quilt on page 80, stitch the small triangles to the short angled strips with a $\frac{1}{4}$ in/0.75 cm seam allowance (**diagram 1**). Press the seams away from the triangles.

diagram 1   diagram 2

2 Again, following the quilt plan carefully, add the long angled strips to the adjacent side of the triangles (**diagram 2**). Note that each triangle has different coloured strips on either side. Press the seams away from the triangles.

3 Sort the triangular patches into piles, separating the triangles pointing upwards from those pointing downwards. Lay out the pieces following the quilt plan. Working from the bottom row, stitch the triangular patches together to form strips (**diagram 3**). On the first and third rows, press the seams to the left. On the second row, press to the right.

diagram 3

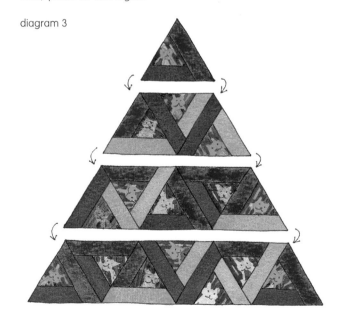

4 Pin the strips together carefully, ensuring the points where seams intersect are lined up correctly. Stitch the strips together. Press the seams flat.

5 Following the plan of the back of the quilt on page 80, stitch the large backing triangles together in the same way as the patches were stitched above. Press.

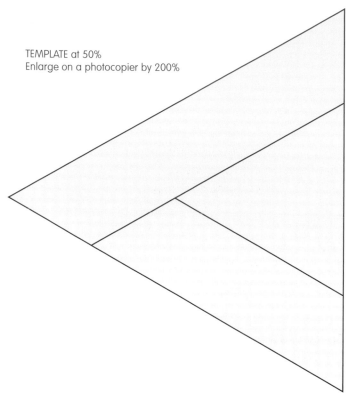

TEMPLATE at 50%
Enlarge on a photocopier by 200%

diagram 5

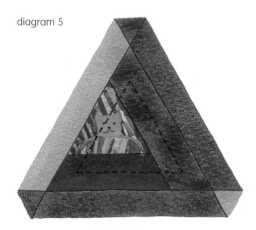

Finishing

1   Spread the backing right side down on a flat surface, then smooth out the wadding and the quilt top, right side up, on top. Fasten together with safety pins or baste in a grid. Tack the layers together along all three axes. Trim the wadding to within $1\frac{3}{4}$ in/4.5 cm of the stitching line **(diagram 4)**.

diagram 4

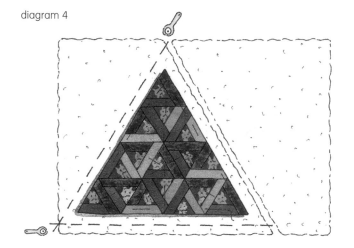

2   To mark the machine quilting lines, line the quilting ruler up, $\frac{7}{8}$ in/2 cm from the edge of the triangular patch and drag a tapestry needle along the ruler. Mark each side of each patch to create a floating triangle in the centre of each large triangle **(diagram 5)**. Machine or hand stitch along the marked lines carefully. Bring all the threads through to the reverse of the quilt, tie off and stitch them in securely.

3   Measure the pieced top along each side, and from each of the red, blue and green border strips, trim one strip to the longest measurement (each side should be approximately the same length).

4   Pin and stitch one of the borders to the front of the quilt, using a $\frac{1}{4}$ in/0.75 cm seam allowance. Stop the stitching $1\frac{3}{4}$ in/4.5 cm from the edge of the wadding at one end. Press under the seam allowance, then pin and tack the border strip to the reverse side. Fold the loose end of the strip back out of the way **(diagram 6)**.

diagram 6

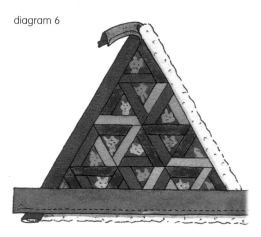

5   Trim the other end of the border strip in line with the wadding. Attach the next strip of border, fold and pin to the reverse side. Fold the border strip around the cut end to create the point of the triangle and trim the other end level with the wadding. Add the final strip so that it goes under the loose end of the first strip.

6   Tack, then handstitch the borders on the reverse side of the quilt. Slip stitch along the edges at each point of the triangle.

Sailboats

Designed by **Mary O'Riordan**

This quilt would make a lovely gift for a summer baby, or the perfect wallhanging for a sunny nursery.

Quilt Plan

Finished size: 42$\frac{1}{2}$ x 32$\frac{1}{2}$ in/108 x 82 cm
Each block is 8 in/20 cm

Materials

All fabrics used in the quilt are 45 in/115 cm wide, 100% cotton.

Sailboat fabrics: 4 in/11 cm each of six different aqua fabrics or scraps to total 24 in/60 cm
For the background, sashing and borders: white, 48 in/1.2 m
For the sashing posts: red and white polka dot, 6 x 8 in/15 x 20 cm
Binding: aqua, blue and red stripe, 20 in/50 cm
Backing: 48 in/1.2 cm fabric of your choice
Wadding: lightweight, 38 x 50 in/96 x 127 cm

Alternative Colour Schemes

1 Blue and white is a natural choice for a nautical theme. Introducing a different colour boat in each block gives a contemporary twist to a traditional colourway.

2 Use soft pinks and peaches as the background for sails in the sunset. This would make a lovely quilt for a little girl sailor!

3 This block is ideal for using up scraps. By varying the fabrics used in the sails, the ships look set for a regatta.

4 It's easy to create a seascape with so many wonderful batiks available to suggest mood and movement.

Cutting

1   From each of the sailboat fabrics, cut four squares measuring $3\frac{3}{8}$ in/8.5 cm.
Cut two rectangles, $2\frac{1}{2}$ x $8\frac{1}{2}$ in/6.5 x 21.5 cm.
Cut two rectangles, $1\frac{1}{2}$ x $8\frac{1}{2}$ in/4.5 x 21.5 cm.

2   From the white background fabric, cut two strips, $3\frac{3}{8}$ in/8.5 cm deep, across the width of the fabric. Cross-cut to produce 24 squares measuring $3\frac{3}{8}$ in/8.5 cm square. Cut two strips, $2\frac{1}{2}$ in/6.5 cm deep, across the width and cross-cut to produce 24 squares measuring $2\frac{1}{2}$ in/ 6.5 cm. Cut three strips, 2 in/5 cm deep, across the width and cross cut into 24 rectangles, 2 x $5\frac{1}{2}$ in/5.5 x 13.5 cm.
Cut two strips, $2\frac{1}{2}$ x $32\frac{1}{2}$ in/6.5 x 82.5 cm and two strips, $2\frac{1}{2}$ x $38\frac{1}{2}$ in/6.5 x 98 cm for the borders. Cut six strips, $2\frac{1}{2}$ in/6.5 cm deep, across the width of the fabric and cross-cut into 17 rectangles, $2\frac{1}{2}$ x $8\frac{1}{2}$ in/6.5 x 21.5 cm, for the sashing strips.

3   From the red and white polka dot fabric, cut six squares measuring $2\frac{1}{2}$ in/6.5 cm for the sashing posts.

4   From the aqua, blue and red stripe fabric, cut eight strips, 2 in/5 cm deep, on the bias for the binding.

Stitching

1   To make one sailboat block, mark a diagonal line on two of the background white $3\frac{3}{8}$ in/8.5 cm squares. Place these two white squares on top of two $3\frac{3}{8}$ in/8.5 cm matching aqua squares with right sides together. Stitch $\frac{1}{4}$ in/0.75 cm on either side of the marked line (**diagram 1**). Cut along the marked line. Press seams towards the aqua fabric.

2   Next, mark a diagonal line on two white 2 in /6.5 cm squares. Place these on either end of a matching aqua $2\frac{1}{2}$ x $8\frac{1}{2}$ in/6.5 x 21.5 cm rectangle, right sides together, with the diagonal line starting at the top left corner on the lefthand square and the top right corner on the right-hand square. Stitch along the marked line (**diagram 2**). Trim the corners $\frac{1}{4}$ in/0.75 cm from the stitching line and press towards the aqua fabric.

diagram 1

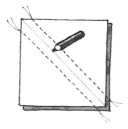

diagram 2

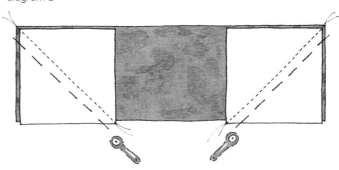

3   Following the block layout in diagram 3, stitch four half-square triangles together to make the sails, then stitch a white 2 x 5½ in/5.5 x 13.5 cm rectangle to each side of the sails. Stitch an aqua and white 2½ x 8½ in/ 6.5 x 21.5 cm rectangle to the bottom to complete the boat, then add a 1½ x 8½ in/4.5 x 21.5 cm matching aqua rectangle at the bottom for the sea. Press towards the darker fabric **(diagram 3)**.

diagram 3

4   Make the other sailboat blocks in the same way, using a different set of aqua fabrics to make a total of 12 blocks.

5   Following the quilt plan on page 86, stitch four rows of three blocks together with a white sashing strip between each block. Stitch the remaining sashing strips together with the red and white sashing posts to make three rows, with three sashing strips and two sashing posts per row.

6   Pin and stitch the four rows of boats together with a sashing strip in between, matching seams carefully.

7   Stitch the 2½ x 38½ in/6.5 x 98 cm border strips to the sides of the quilt. Press towards the border fabric. Stitch the remaining two border strips to the top and bottom of the quilt and press towards the border fabric.

Finishing

1   Spread the backing right side down on a flat surface, then smooth out the wadding and the patchwork top, right side up, on top. Fasten together with safety pins or baste in a grid.

2   Quilt in-the-ditch along the sashing lines and around the sailing boats ¼ in/0.75 cm from the seam lines.

3   Join the binding strips with diagonal seams to make a continuous length to fit all round the quilt and use to bind the edges with a double-fold binding, mitred at the corners.

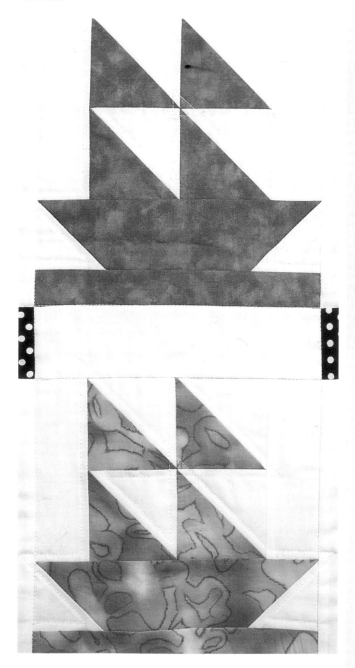

Spotty Zigzag Bed Quilt

Designed by **Alison Wood**

Bright spots and primary plain fabrics make this first bed quilt for a toddler really lively. The simple four-patch blocks are arranged vertically by colour in the manner of a traditional strippy quilt, but interest and movement are added by the lines of blocks being offset to create the blue zigzags down the length of the quilt, emphasized by the simple machine quilting.

Quilt Plan

Finished size: 97 x 69 in/247 x 175 cm
Finished four-patch block size: 7 in/17 cm square

Materials

All fabrics used in the quilt top are 45 in/115 cm wide, 100% cotton.

Four-patch blocks: spotty fabric, 12 in/30 cm and plain fabric, 12 in/30 cm per vertical row. As this quilt has seven rows, if you want each row to be different you will need seven different spotty fabrics and seven different plain fabrics.
Setting triangles: plain blue, 4½ yds/4 m
Backing: 6 yds/5.25 m in colour of your choice
Binding: 24 in/70 cm in colour of your choice or join together strips from the leftover block fabrics to make a colourful pieced binding
Wadding: 108 x 90 in/275 x 227 cm (twin bed size), cotton or 80:20 cotton/polyester mix for machine quilting. For hand quilting use either cotton/cotton blend or 2 oz polyester.

Alternative Colour Schemes

1 Pastel squares pick out colours from the multicoloured setting triangle fabric.

2 Choose flannels for a cozy, country looking quilt.

3 Antique reproduction fabrics are showcased in the four-patch blocks.

4 The design offers an opportunity to feature the diverse styles and textures of batiks.

Note:
Be wary of using strongly directional or striped fabrics for this quilt, particularly in the setting triangles, and only choose plaids if you like a relaxed "off-grain" look.

Cutting

1   For the four-patch blocks, cut two strips 4 in/10 cm deep across the width of each of the plain and spotty fabrics.

2   From the blue fabric for the side setting triangles, cut twelve strips, 11¼ in/26.5 cm deep, across the width of the fabric. Cross-cut into 36 x 11¼ in/26.5 cm squares (each strip should yield three squares).
Cut 32 of the squares in half along both diagonals to give 128 quarter-square triangles. Cut the remaining three squares in half along one diagonal to give six half-square triangles.
Cut two 6 in/14 cm strips and cross-cut into eight 6 in/14 cm squares. Cut these squares in half once diagonally to make 16 half-square triangles. These small setting triangles will be used for setting the top and bottom of the odd-numbered rows of the quilt.

3   From the binding fabric, cut nine strips, 2½ in/6 cm deep, across the width of the fabric.

4   Cut the backing fabric in half crosswise.

Stitching

1   For each set of four-patch blocks, stitch together one strip of spotty and one strip of plain fabric, right sides together, along the length of the strips, taking a ¼ in/0.75 cm seam allowance. Repeat with the other strips in this set. Chain piecing the strips will save time and thread. Be consistent about the direction in which you press your seam allowances: for example, always press towards the spotty fabric.

NOTE
Careful attention to pressing at this stage will give accurate blocks which will in turn help with accurate piecing of the triangles. Press the seams joining the strips flat first with the strips right sides together; this "sets" the seam, causing the thread to sink into the fabric a little to give a flat, crisp finish. Use the side of the iron to open the top strip, pressing from the right side to ensure there are no little pleats beside the seams. Press, rather than iron the fabric to avoid curving the stitched strip set.

2   Place one pair of stitched strips on top of another pair of stitched strips of the same fabric combination, so that the spotty fabric is on top of the plain and vice versa.

Cross-cut the strips into rectangles each 4 in/10 cm wide (**diagram 1**). Repeat with all the remaining strips in this colourway. You should be able to cut at least ten pairs.

diagram 1

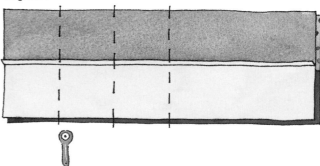

3   Stitch each pair of rectangles together down one long side with the seam allowance on top facing towards the needle: this helps the seam allowances to butt together giving a well-matched point in the centre of the four-patch block.

4   Press the seams closed to set them. Hold a four-patch block with the wrong side facing you and with the horizontal seam allowance pointing away from you. Pull the section of seam allowance on the right hand side of the patch towards you with your right thumb whilst keeping the left hand seam allowance pushed away from you: the few stitches in the seam allowance should "pop" open,

allowing the seams to lie in opposite directions, which reduces bulk in the centre of the block (**diagram 2**). Press the completed unit from the wrong side, and again from the right side.

diagram 2

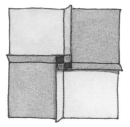

NOTE

I am grateful to Harriet Hargrave, inspirational American quiltmaker and teacher, for showing me this seam allowance technique; it is very easy to do provided your stitch length isn't too short, and really reduces the bulk in the centre of the block, which makes quilting much easier.

5   Repeat steps 1 to 4 for each of the other colourways chosen, until you have ten blocks for each of the seven vertical rows of the quilt. You will only need nine blocks for the even-numbered rows but making ten of each colourway gives you more choice when laying out the design.

6   Following the quilt plan on page 92, lay out the blocks, alternating the direction of the spotty fabric in each row to add interest.

7   Stitch two side setting triangles to opposite sides of each four-patch block. Stitch with the triangle on top, from the square corner towards the triangle point (**diagrams 3 and 4**). Press the seam allowance towards the triangle. The blocks at the top and bottom of the odd-numbered rows should have only one side setting triangle.

diagram 3

diagram 4

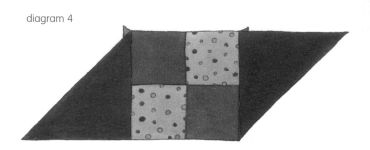

8   Join the blocks into pairs and then rows, matching seams carefully. The seam allowances should butt together in opposite directions (**diagram 5**). Press the seams in one direction, as convenient.

diagram 5

9 Referring to the quilt plan again, lay out the rows. The even-numbered rows that contain only nine blocks are finished with a large half-square setting triangle (**diagram 6**). Stitch one of these triangles to the top and bottom of each even-numbered row and press well.

diagram 6

diagram 7

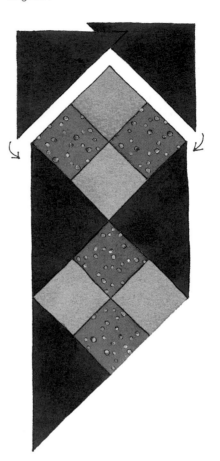

diagram 8

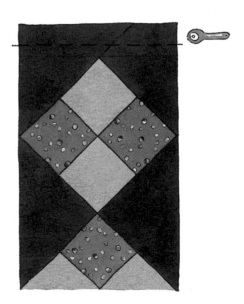

10 Complete the odd-numbered rows at the top and bottom with the small setting triangles cut from the 6 in/14 cm squares (**diagram 7**). The setting triangles are generously sized and you may find that, when all the setting triangles have been added and the strips carefully pressed, you wish to trim away some of the excess fabric: remember to leave a $^1/_4$ in/0.75 cm seam allowance beyond the point of the last four-patch block in the strip (**diagram 8**).

11 Following the quilt plan, stitch the seven rows together. To do this, pinch a crease or mark with a pin halfway along the edge of each setting triangle and line up with the point of the four-patch block in the adjoining row. Pin along the length of the row and stitch. Take care not to "cut off" the points of the four-patch blocks by stitching too wide a seam. Set the seams, then press the seam allowances between the rows open to reduce bulk.

12 When all the rows have been joined, press the top well.

Finishing

1 Trim the selvages from the two backing pieces and join together down the longer sides – the seam will run vertically across the quilt. Press the seam open.

2 Spread the backing right side down on a flat surface, then smooth out the wadding and the patchwork top, right side up, on top. Fasten together with safety pins or baste in a grid.

3 Mark the top with your chosen quilting design. The quilt shown was quilted in-the-ditch around the four-patch blocks, then in four long zigzag lines $1/2$ in/1.5 cm apart and parallel to the edge of the blocks. This emphasizes the vertical design of the quilt and helps to make the blocks stand out. The same parallel lines of stitching were repeated in the setting triangles around the outside edges of the quilt.

4 Use the binding strips to make a double-fold binding, mitred at the corners.

Random Patch Bed Quilt

Designed by **Rita Whitehorn**

The method used here is a modern version of the crazy patchwork theme. The pieces are cut to a uniform size but in varying depths, then pieced together in strips with broderie anglaise embellishment. It's a showcase for all those lovely white-on-white fabrics and makes a lovely first bed quilt.

Quilt Plan

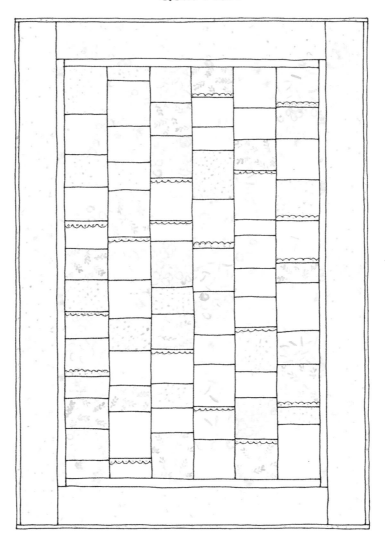

Finished size: 100 x 70 in/254 x 179 cm

Materials

All fabrics used in this quilt are 45 in/115 cm wide, 100% cotton.

Outer borders and binding: white-on-white print, 3 yds/2.6 m
Central blocks: Three different white-on-white prints, ¹/₂ yd/50 cm/23 cm of each and another three different white-on-white prints, ³/₄ yd/70 cm of each
Central blocks and inner borders: an eighth white-on-white print, 1¹/₃ yds/1.3 m
Broderie anglaise: 2¹/₂ yds/2.3 m, 2 in/5 cm wide, and 2¹/₂ yds/2.3 m, 1 in/2.5 cm wide
Backing: white-on-white print, 5 yds 28 in/5.3 m
Quilting thread: white
Medium lead pencil or quilt marking pencil
Wadding: lightweight, 104 x 74 in/264 x 189 cm

Alternative Colour Schemes

The broderie anglaise embellishment makes this quilt design more suitable for a little girl, so the following fabrics all reflect that.

1 A bright mixture of soft colours makes a sunny colour scheme.

2 Happy animal prints teamed with strong pastels give a lively colourway.

3 Match the soft pastels of the novelty prints with other small print fabrics for a very pretty colourway.

4 A harmonious mix of creams, pale yellow and orange with a touch of blue for interest.

Cutting

1 From the outer border and binding fabric, cut two strips, each 7 in/18.5 cm wide, down the length of the fabric and two strips, each 7 x 57 in/18.5 x 145 cm, down the length for the outer borders. Cut four strips, 2½ in/6.5 cm wide, down the length for the binding.

2 From the central block and inner border fabric, cut 7 strips, 2¾ in/7.5 cm deep, across the width for the inner borders.

3 From the remaining white-on-white fabrics for the central blocks and from the broderie anglaise or eyelet lace, cut assorted pieces each 9 in/23 cm wide and to various depths. Arrange as you cut, following the quilt plan to make six block panels each approximately 9 x 88½ in/23 x 225 cm before stitching the seams. Insert the broad and narrow broderie anglaise over one or two of the pieces. Diagram 1 shows how I arranged the lefthand strip but the idea is to put the pieces together randomly and without needing to cut accurately.

4 Cut the backing fabric in half crosswise, then rejoin the two pieces down one long side to make a piece 104 x 74 in/264 x 189 cm.

diagram 1

Stitching

1 Top stitch the broderie anglaise fabric in position first, then stitch the blocks together in six columns. Pin and stitch the columns together to make one centre panel approximately 51½ x 82 in/130.5 x 205 cm.

2 To add the inner border, take three of the 2¾ in/7.5 cm border strips, cut one in half and join one half to each of the other two. Stitch to the top and bottom of the pieced top and trim as necessary. Press seams towards the borders.

3 Take the remaining four border strips and join in pairs. Stitch to the sides and trim as necessary. Press as before.

4 To add the outer border, measure the pieced top through the centre from side to side, then trim the two shorter 7 in/18.5 cm border strips to this measurement. Stitch to the top and bottom of the quilt. Press seams towards the darker fabric.

5 Measure the pieced top through the centre from top to bottom, then trim the two longer border strips to this measurement. Stitch to the sides of the quilt and press as before.

Finishing

1 Spread the backing right side down on a flat surface, then smooth out the wadding and the patchwork top, right side up, on top. Fasten together with safety pins or baste in a grid.

2 Use white quilting thread to quilt in-the-ditch at random between patches. Quilt in-the-ditch between the inner and outer border and between the outer border and binding.

3 Press all the binding strips in half, right sides facing outwards along the length of the fabric.

4 Pin one of the longer binding strips along one side of the quilt, aligning raw edges. Trim to fit and stitch taking the usual seam allowance. Fold to the back and hem stitch in place along the stitching line. Repeat on the opposite side.

5 For the top and bottom, stitch the two shorter strips to the quilt in the same way but before folding to the back, trim the strips so that they are $1/4$ in/0.75 cm longer than the quilt at each end. Fold in the short overlap, then fold the binding to the back and hem stitch in place.

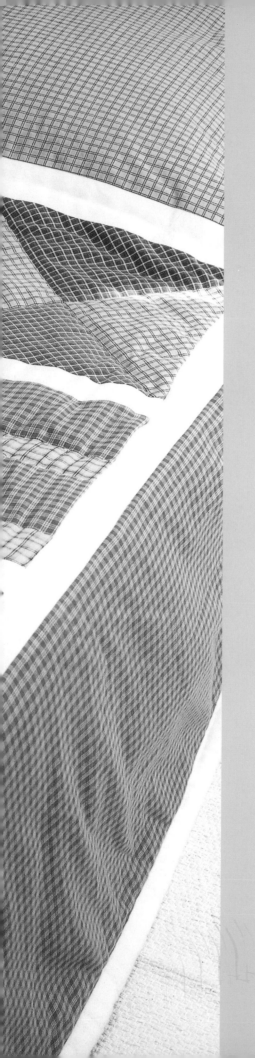

Play on Plaids

Designed by **Rita Whitehorn**

These soft flannels make a wonderfully warm first bed quilt for a toddler. The design, with its twelve individual block patterns, is a simple version of a sampler quilt. The large borders compensate for the time taken to stitch the blocks.

Quilt Plan

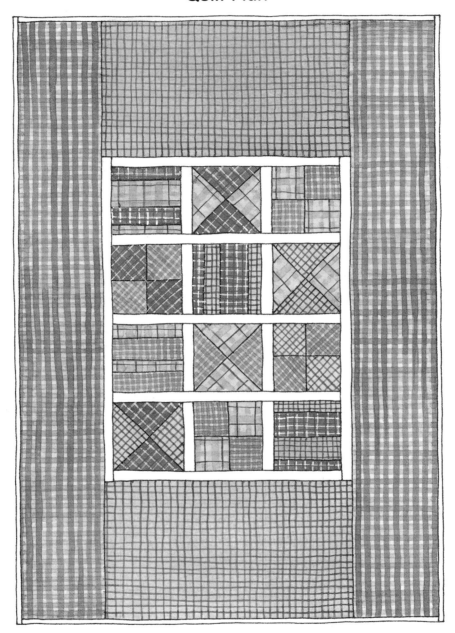

Finished size: 100 x 69 in/250 x 175 cm

Materials

All fabrics used in this quilt are 45 in/115 cm wide, 100% cotton flannel.

Central blocks and side borders: green check flannel, 3 yds/2.7 m
Central blocks and top/bottom borders: pink check flannel, 2 yds/1.8 m
Central blocks: yellow check flannel, 30 in/75 cm; blue check flannel, 20 in/50 cm
Sashing and binding: cream flannel, 2¹/₃ yds/2.2 m
Wadding: 104 x 73 in/260 x 185 cm
Backing: 5 yds 28 in/5.3 m fabric
Pearl cotton: cream, pink and green to match the fabrics

Alternative Colour Schemes

1 Start with bold novelty prints for the borders and pick out plain and small prints fabrics for the central blocks to make a great first quilt for a little boy.
2 Pick out a moon and stars novelty print for the borders and a mixture of plain and starry fabrics for the blocks.
3 Teddy bear prints are always popular – match with plain or small print fabrics for the blocks, so that the quilt is not too busy.
4 Soft pastel fairy prints matched with plain pastels for the blocks make a pretty colour scheme for a little girl.

Cutting

1 From the green check fabric, cut two strips, 13 x 100 in/34 x 250 cm, down the length of the fabric. Cut one strip, 6½ x 52 in/16.5 x 132 cm, down the length and cross-cut into 8 squares. Cut two rectangles, 12½ x 4½ in/31.5 x 11.5 cm. Cut one square, 13¾ in/35 cm, and cross-cut into two triangles along the diagonal.

2 From the pink check fabric, cut two strips, 21½ x 44½ in/54 x 111.5 cm, down the length of the fabric. Cut two squares, 13¾ in/35 cm, and cross-cut each one into two triangles along the diagonal. Cut two rectangles, 2½ x 12½ in/6.5 x 31.5 cm. Cut one rectangle, 3½ x 12½ in/ 9 x 31.5 cm; cut one rectangle, 4½ x 12½ in/11.5 x 31.5 cm; cut one rectangle, 6½ x 13 in/16.5 x 33 cm.

3 From the yellow check fabric, cut one strip, 13¾ in/35 cm deep, across the width of the fabric and cross-cut into three squares. Cut two rectangles, 6½ x 13 in/16.5 x 33 cm, and cross-cut into four squares. Cut one rectangle, 5½ x 12½ in/14 x 31.5 cm, and three rectangles, 2½ x 12½ in/6.5 x 31.5 cm.

4 From the blue check fabric, cut two squares, 13¾ in/35 cm wide. Cut two rectangles, 2½ x 12½ in/6.5 x 31.5 cm. Cut one rectangle, 3½ x 12½ in/9 x 31.5 cm; cut one rectangle, 4½ x 12½in/11.5 x 31.5 cm; cut one rectangle, 6½ x 13 in/16.5 x 33 cm and cross-cut into two squares.

5 From the cream sashing and binding fabric, cut two strips, 2½ x 58½ in/6.5 x 146.5 cm, down the length of the fabric. Cut five strips, 2½ x 40 ½ in/6.5 x 101.5 cm, down the length and eight rectangles, 2½ x 12½ in/6.5 x 31.5 cm. Cut nine strips, 2½ in/6.5 cm deep, across the width of the fabric for the binding.

6 Cut the backing fabric in two across the width.

Stitching

1 There are three different types of blocks made up of strips, triangles and squares, each in a different colour combination (diagram 1). To stitch the first strippy block, take one blue 2½ x 12½ in/6.5 x 31.5 cm rectangle and place right sides together with a yellow 5½ x 12½ in/ 14 x 31.5 cm rectangle. Stitch together down one long side taking a ¼ in/0.75 cm seam allowance. Press the seam towards the blue fabric. Stitch a 3½ x 12½ in/ 9 x 31.5 cm blue rectangle to the bottom of the yellow strip in the same way. Then complete the block by stitching a 2½ x 12½ in/6.5 x 31.5 cm yellow rectangle to the bottom of the blue strip.

2 Repeat step one to make three more strip blocks, made up of the following 12½ in/31.5 cm strips: 2½ in/6.5 cm blue + 3½ in/9 cm pink + 5½ in/14 cm blue + 2½ in/6.5 cm pink;

diagram 1

2½ in/6.5 cm yellow + 4½ in/11.5 cm green + 2½ in/
6.5 cm yellow + 4½ in/11.5 cm green;
2½ in/6.5 cm pink + 4½ in/11.5 cm blue + 4½ in/11.5 cm
pink + 2½ in/6.5 cm blue.

3   To stitch the first triangle block, place one blue
triangle right sides together with one yellow triangle,
matching straight edges. Stitch taking the usual seam
allowance. Press towards the darker fabric. Repeat with a
second pair of blue and yellow triangles, then place the
two units just stitched right sides together and stitch
down the long side.

4   Repeat to make three further triangle blocks using the
following combinations:
pink and yellow triangles; yellow and green triangles; pink
and blue triangles.

5   To stitch the first four-square block, place one yellow
6½ in/16.5 cm square right sides together with one
green 6½ in/16.5 cm square and stitch, taking the usual
seam allowance. Press towards the darker fabric. Repeat
with a second pair of green and yellow squares, then
place the two units just stitched right sides together and
stitch down the long side.

6   Repeat to make three further four-square blocks using
the following combinations:
blue and green squares; pink and green squares; yellow
and green squares.

7   Lay out the twelve blocks just made in four rows of
three blocks following the quilt plan on page 106. Stitch
each row of blocks together with a 2½ x 12½ in/6.5 x
31.5 cm sashing strip in between **(diagram 2)**.

diagram 2

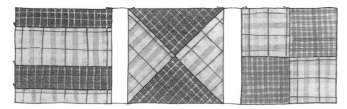

8   Join the four rows with a 2½ x 40½ in/6.5 x 101.5 cm
sashing strip in between and add one to the top and
bottom of the panel just created.

9   Stitch a 2½ x 58½ in/6.5 x 146.5 cm sashing strip on
either side of the central panel.

Adding the Borders

1   Pin and stitch one pink 21½ x 44½ in/54 x 111.5 cm
strip to the top of the central panel and repeat to stitch
the remaining pink strip to the bottom.

2   Pin and stitch one green 13 x 100 in/34 x 250 cm strip
to one side of the central panel and repeat to stitch the
remaining green strip to the other side.

Finishing

1   Stitch the two backing pieces together down one long
side and trim to make a piece 104 x 73 in/260 x 185 cm.

2   Spread the backing fabric right side down on a flat
surface, then smooth out the wadding and the patchwork
top, right side up, on top. Fasten together with safety
pins or baste in a grid.

3   Using big stitch quilting and cream pearl cotton, hand
quilt in-the-ditch along all the seams within the blocks
and down the middle of the sashing strips. Using pearl
cotton to match the fabrics, extend the quilting lines from
the sashing into the borders and finally quilt a line
through the centre of the pink borders at the top and
bottom of the quilt. When the quilting is finished, trim
the edges.

4   Join the nine binding strips into one long length. Press
in half, wrong sides together along the length of the fabric.

5   Measure the pieced top through the centre from top to
bottom, then cut two strips to this measurement from the
binding strip. Pin one of the strips along one side of the
quilt, aligning raw edges. Stitch taking the usual seam
allowance. Fold to the back and hem stitch in place along
the stitching line. Repeat on the opposite side.

6   Measure the pieced top through the centre from side
to side, then cut two strips to this measurement plus
½ in/1.5 cm from the remaining binding strip. Pin
centrally to the top and bottom of the quilt and stitch as
above but before folding to the back, fold in the short
overlap at either end, then fold the binding to the back
and hem stitch in place.

THE CONTRIBUTORS

Janet Goddard writes patterns for magazines and books and teaches patchwork across Hertfordshire, Essex and North London.

Mary O'Riordan is an experienced quiltmaker who works at "The Quilt Room" in Dorking, Surrey

Gail Smith opened her shop, "Abigail Crafts", after completing a City and Guild course; she is a qualified adult education teacher, running local patchwork groups.

Sarah Wellfair is a qualified teacher who runs a full programme of workshops from her patchwork shop, "Goose Chase Quilting", at Leckhampton in Gloucestershire.

Rita Whitehorn is an experienced quiltmaker and designer, who makes quilts to commission.

Rosemary Wilkinson is an experienced quiltmaker and craft book editor, specialising in books on patchwork quilting.

Alison Wood teaches patchwork and quilting classes and works part-time at "The Quilt Room" in Dorking, Surrey.

Dorothy Wood is an author and designer who has written and contributed to over twenty needlecraft books.

SUPPLIERS

UK

Abigail Crafts
3-5 Regent Street
Stonehouse
Gloucestershire GL10 2AA
Tel: 01453 823691
www.abigailcrafts.co.uk
Patchwork and embroidery supplies

The Bramble Patch
West Street
Weedon
Northants NN7 4QU
Tel: 01327 342212
Patchwork and quilting supplies

The Cotton Patch
1285 Stratford Road
Hall Green
Birmingham B28 9AJ
Tel: 0121 702 2840
Patchwork and quilting supplies

Creative Quilting
3 Bridge Road
East Molesey
Surrey KT8 9EU
Tel: 020 8941 7075
Specialist retailer

Custom Quilting Limited
"Beal na Tra"
Derrymihan West
Castletownbere
Co Cork, Eire
Email: patches@iol.ie
Long arm quilting services

Fred Aldous Ltd
P.O Box 135
37 Lever Street
Manchester M1 1LW
Tel: 0161 236 2477
Mail order craft materials

Goose Chase Quilting
65 Great Norwood Street
Leckhampton
Cheltenham GL50 2BQ
Tel: 01242 512639
Patchwork and quilting supplies

Hab-bits
Unit 9, Vale Business Park
Cowbridge
Vale of Glamorgan
CF71 7PF
Tel: 01446 775150
Haberdashery supplies

Patchwork Direct
c/o Heirs & Graces
King Street
Bakewell
Derbyshire DE45 1DZ
Tel: 01629 815873
www.patchworkdirect.com
Patchwork and quilting supplies

Purely Patchwork
23 High Street
Linlithgow
West Lothian
Scotland
Tel: 01506 846200
Patchwork and quilting supplies

The Quilt Loft
9/10 Havercroft Buildings
North Street
Worthing
West Sussex BN11 1DY
Tel: 01903 233771
Quilt supplies, classes and workshops

The Quilt Room
20 West Street
Dorking
Surrey RH4 1BL
Tel: 01306 740739
www.quiltroom.co.uk
Quilt supplies, classes and workshops

Mail order: The Quilt Room
c/o Carvilles
Station Road
Dorking
Surrey RH4 1XH
Tel: 01306 877307

Quilting Solutions
Firethorn
Rattlesden Road
Drinkstone
Bury St Edmunds
Suffolk IP30 9TL
Tel: 01449 735280
Email: firethorn@lineone.net
www.quiltingsolutions.co.uk
Long arm quilting services

The Sewing Shed
Shanahill West
Keel
Castlemaine
Co Kerry, Eire
Tel: 00 35366 9766931
www.thesewingshed@eir-
com.net
Patchwork and quilting
supplies

Stitch in Time
293 Sandycombe Road
Kew
Surrey TW9 3LU
Tel: 020 8948 8462
www.stitchintimeuk.com
Specialist quilting retailer

Strawberry Fayre
Chagford
Devon TQ13 8EN
Tel: 01647 433250
Mail order fabrics and quilts

Sunflower Fabrics
157-159 Castle Road
Bedford MK40 3RS
Tel: 01234 273819
www.sunflowerfabrics.com
Quilting supplies

Worn and Washed
The Walled Garden
48 East Street
Olney
Bucks MK 46 4DW
Tel: 01234 240881
Email:kim@wornandwashed-
fabrics.com

South Africa

Crafty Supplies
Stadium on Main
Main Road
Claremont 7700
Tel: 021 671 0286
Fern Gully
46 3rd Street
Linden
2195
Tel: 011 782 7941

Nimble Fingers
Shop 222
Kloof Village Mall
Village Road
Kloof 3610
Tel: 031 764 6283

Pied Piper
69 1st Avenue
Newton Park
Port Elizabeth 6001
Tel: 041 365 1616

Quilt Talk
40 Victoria Street
George 6530
Tel: 044 873 2947

Quilt Tech
9 Louanna Avenue
Kloofendal
Extension 5 1709
Tel: 011 679 4386

Quilting Supplies
42 Nellnapius Drive
Irene 0062
Tel: 012 667 2223

Simply Stitches
2 Topaz Street
Albernarle
Germiston 1401
Tel: 011 902 6997

Stitch 'n' Stuff
140 Lansdowne Road
Claremont 7700
Tel: 021 674 4059

Australia

Country Patchwork Cottage
10/86 Erindale Road
Balcatta
WA 6021
Tel: (08) 9345 3550
The Quilters Store
22 Shaw Street
Auchenflower
QLD 4066
Tel: (07) 3870 0408

Patchwork of Essendon
96 Fletcher Street
Essendon
VIC 3040
Tel: (03) 9372 0793

Patchwork Plus
Shop 81
7-15 Jackson Avenue
Miranda
NSW 2228
Tel: (02) 9540 278

Quilts and Threads
827 Lower North East Road
Dernancourt
SA 5075
Tel: (08) 8365 6711

Riverlea Cottage Quilts
Shop 4, 330 Unley Road
Hyde Park
SA 5061
Tel: (08) 8373 0653

New Zealand

Grandmothers Garden
Patchwork and Quilting
1042 Gordonton Road
Gordonton
Hamilton
Tel: (07) 824 3050

**Hands Ashford Craft Supply
Store**
5 Normans Road
Christchurch
Tel: (03) 355 9099
www.hands.co.nz

Needlecraft Distributors
600 Main Street
Palmerston North
Tel: (06) 356 4793
Fax: (06) 355 4594

Patchwork Barn
132 Hinemoa Street
Birkenhead
Auckland
Tel: (09) 480 5401

The Patchwork Shop
356 Grey Street
Hamilton
Tel: (07) 856 6365

The Quilt Shop
35 Pearn Place
Northcote Shopping Centre
Auckland
Tel: (09) 480 0028
Fax: (09) 480 0380

Spotlight Stores
Whangarei (09) 430 7220
Wairau Park (09) 444 0220
Henderson (09) 836 0888
Panmure (09) 527 0915
Manukau City (09) 263 6760
Hamilton (07) 839 1793
Rotorua (07) 343 6901
New Plymouth (06) 757 3575
Gisborne (06) 863 0037
Hastings (06) 878 5223
Palmerston North (06) 357
6833
Porirua (04) 238 4055
Wellington (04) 472 5600
Christchurch (03) 377 6121
Dunedin (03) 477 1478
www.spotlight.net.nz

Stitch and Craft
32 East Tamaki Road
Papatoetoe
Auckland
Tel: (09) 278 1351
Fax: (09) 278 1356

Stitches
351 Colombo Street
Christchurch
Tel: (03) 379 1868
Fax: (03) 377 2347
www.stitches.co.nz

Variety Handcrafts
106 Princes Street
Dunedin
Tel: (03) 474 1088

INDEX